Delia Ha_____

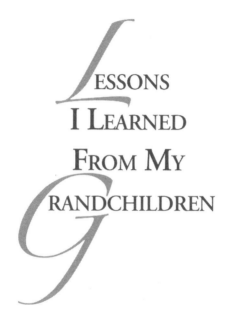

LESSONS
I LEARNED
FROM MY
GRANDCHILDREN

DIMENSIONS
FOR LIVING

NASHVILLE

LESSONS I LEARNED FROM MY GRANDCHILDREN

Copyright © 2008 by Dimensions for Living

This book is printed on acid-free paper.

Library of Congress Cataloging-in-Publication Data

Halverson, Delia Touchton.
  Dimensions for living : lessons I learned from my grandchildren / Delia Halverson.
    p. cm.
  ISBN 978-0-687-65078-1 (binding: pbk. : alk. paper)
  1. Grandparents—Prayers and devotions. 2. Grandparent and child—Religious aspects—Christianity. I. Title.
BV4845.H35 2008
242'—60853—dc22

                                                                2007042432

All Scripture quotations in this publication, unless otherwise noted, are from the Contemporary English Version Copyright © 1991, 1992, 1995 by American Bible Society, Used by Permission.

Scripture quotations marked NRSV are from the New Revised Standard Version of the Bible, copyright 1989, Division of Christian Education of the National Council of the Churches of Christ in the United States of America. Used by permission. All rights reserved.

Selections from "Lessons on Help Requests" were previously published in Delia Halverson, *Living Simply, Simply Living* (Nashville: Abingdon Press, 1996). Out of print.

08 09 10 11 12 13 14 15 16 17—10 9 8 7 6 5 4 3 2 1

MANUFACTURED IN THE UNITED STATES OF AMERICA

Lessons I Learned from My Grandchildren

Contents

Introduction

A little background into our family may help you better understand these reflections. My husband, Sam, and I are blessed with four delightful grandchildren. Jesse and Megan live ten hours away from us, and Mya and Lea, twin girls, live right across the street. Our daughter adopted the twins when they were four days old. Since she is a single mom, Sam and I have kept the twins every day that their mother has taught since they were ten weeks old. I realize now how much I missed by living a distance from our other two grandchildren when they were very young. But all four of our grandchildren have taught me many lessons.

The lessons from my grandchildren have not all come from their conscious wisdom. Usually they have no idea that I've gained insight from them. Sometimes the wisdom comes because their actions or words spurred me to do my own thinking. Sometimes there isn't even any wisdom, but only a gentle prodding to set my mind to thinking and maybe to do a little questioning on my own. But these times are lessons, nonetheless. These are the times when God has used these dear children to help me grow in my own faith.

Whether you have grandchildren of your own, or whether you just have opportunities to be with children, I hope the simple reflections will prod you to think through your relationship with God and with children. You will realize that, as Jesus said, unless we become as a little child we will never know the fullness of the true potential of our relationship with God.

LESSONS OF EXPERIENCES AND JOYS

Lessons of Each Special Day

Scripture: *All of you nations, clap your hands and shout joyful praises to God.*

—Psalm 47:1

Our twin granddaughters learned early on, even before they could talk, to express their joy with clapping. They clapped when they saw someone they knew. They clapped when they accomplished something new. They clapped when a special show came on television. They clapped when their grandfather put their favorite dish on the table. (He cooks the main meals at our house!) And they clapped when we sang praise to God.

When the girls first sat in high chairs for their meals, I began singing a special song to them at breakfast. It uses the words of Psalm 118:24 (NRSV): "This is the day that the LORD has made; let us rejoice and be glad in it." Even though they did not understand the meaning of the words, they knew that it was a song of joy, and they reacted with their clapping. Even now, when we sing the song, they immediately break out in smiles and cheers accompanied with spontaneous clapping.

Each day with grandchildren is special. I never know just what it will hold. It may be the day that they learn a new word, such as *floor* or *dinosaur*. Or it may be the day that they accomplish a special dance step or a complicated karate move. Or it may simply be another day with the same games and toys. But nonetheless, it is special to them, and I'm finding it special to me.

Once we are adults we get hung up in busyness. Life is a rush from one job to another, from one meeting to another, or from one relationship to another. We not only forget to clap for joy over the simple accomplishments, but we forget to recognize each day as a day that God has made and a day that we live for God.

If slowing down with grandchildren does nothing more, it can teach us to find joy in each day. It can teach us that there are ordinary things in life to celebrate, as well as the extra-ordinary. It can teach us an awareness that we have forgotten in our "maturity." It can teach us to feel unashamed about celebrating with joy and with excitement—celebrating the specialness of today and the specialness of relationships!

Reflect
~ What happened today that you can clap about?
~ Besides clapping, what other ways can you celebrate the joy of a moment?
~ How can you find a way to remind yourself of the many moments that are special?

Pray
God, you have given us days, some routine and some unusual. Help me see the specialness of each day. Help me lose all my reluctance of celebrating your gifts of new days. Amen.

Lessons of Laughter

Scripture: And a little child shall lead them.
—Isaiah 11:6c (NRSV)

It is a joy to watch my grandchildren in some of their antics. At times I simply smile inside and try not to burst into laughter, because they would not think it was a laughing matter. Other times I laugh with them, feeling the explosion of endorphins through my body. And then there are times when I laugh until my sides hurt and tears spill over and down my cheeks!

Research indicates that endorphins make a difference in our physical and emotional health. When was the last time you really laughed until the tears ran down your face? Perhaps laughter is one reason children tend to be more physically fit than we adults. It is estimated that children laugh an average of four hundred times a day, while we adults laugh only about fifteen times a day. What a difference! Where did we adults lose it? Why can't we follow children's leading and remember to laugh more frequently?

There are other areas where we can follow children's leadership and make our lives more meaningful. Here are some suggestions:

- Look for the little things: select one square foot of ground, and write down everything you see in that square.
- Start out for a walk with no destination in mind, and let your interest in your surroundings lead you.

- Take off your shoes and splash through the next rain shower.
- Investigate different items in nature just to enjoy their different textures.
- Run in circles with a puppy or a child.
- Fly a kite or hug a tree.
- Ride a bike or open the windows of the car and feel the wind in your face.
- Walk through the grass barefoot, and giggle as the grass tickles your toes.

Most important of all, take the example of children who learn from their mistakes and simply get up and try it again. Bad past experiences cannot be changed. If we don't use them to learn, then they make us miserable as we continually bring them to mind. Learning from our mistakes makes them worthwhile. Laughing about them buffs the sharp edges, so that we can hold them in our hands and find the kernel of learning inside.

Reflect

~ Count the number of times you laughed in the past twenty-four hours. How can you increase your laughter time?

~ When have you put everything on hold and enjoyed an adventure as you did as a child?

~ What past experience can you use to learn from and laugh about, instead of regretting or cursing it?

Pray

Dear God, through children you give us examples of a joyful life. Help us follow the leading of our children and appreciate all the opportunities of life. Amen.

Lessons of Quiet Times

Scripture: But so many people were coming and going that Jesus and the apostles did not even have a chance to eat. Then Jesus said, "Let's go to a place where we can be alone and get some rest."

—Mark 6:31

Grandchildren seem to have boundless energy, particularly the younger ones. How often we say, "If I could bottle that energy and sell it, I'd be a billionaire." Older grandchildren don't always exhibit their energy, yet they may have the energy to go to a party and dance most of the night away. Which brings me to the lesson I've learned from my grandchildren about quiet times. We all need some "downtime." It may come in the form of exhausted sleep or it may come as a simple time of reflection within ourselves.

As I've cared for my little twin granddaughters, I've come to recognize that when they become irritable, they are actually tired and are not getting the sleep they need. Their good spirits and happy smiles usually return when they have adequate sleep.

God created our bodies in such a manner that we must have sleep or we will become ill. If God is all-powerful, as we believe, then God could have created us so that we did not need sleep. Consequently I see sleep as a true gift from God. Sleep is our Creator's way of saying, "Relax; rest in my care and renew yourself for tomorrow."

Jesus exhibited another way to rest. He often drew away to be by himself and pray. The humanness of Jesus required that time of quiet reflection. When we go day after day without drawing apart to spend quiet time with God, then in essence we are saying that our spiritual lives are stronger than that of Jesus, and that we don't need renewal as Jesus did. I think not. I think that we have revved up our lives so much that we fool ourselves into thinking we don't need quiet times. We fill our ears with music, our eyes with images, and our stomachs with food. We fool ourselves into thinking that fullness is good.

After a recent vacation away from grandchildren, I returned to learn again that emptiness is good because it allows us to fill ourselves. On that day I simply sat in a chair and held two grandchildren quietly. We basked in our love for each other. There was no talking, no wiggling, no energy expended. We simply loved and received love.

How like our time with God. Someone has said that time with God is like simply "looking and loving." We need time without asking God for anything, without complaining to God, without even thanking God. We need time just to be with God and to "look and love."

Reflect

~ When was the last time you simply spent time with God "looking and loving"?

~ What can you cull from your life in order to have more time to appreciate aloneness with God?

~ How can you help children find time to empty themselves and be filled with God?

Pray

Creator God, thank you for making us with the need for rest. Help me realize that I need the rest, not only for my physical body but also for my spiritual being. Amen.

Lessons of the Wonders of God's World

Scripture: I often think of the heavens your hands have made, and of the moon and stars you put in place.
Then I ask, "Why do you care about us humans?
Why are you concerned for us weaklings?"

—Psalm 8:3-4

God's world gives us so many times to wonder and reflect. We take that world for granted, skipping over the violet growing between the cracks in the sidewalk and stepping on the ant that could teach us great lessons of life.

If we pay attention to our young grandchildren we will learn again to wonder over these things. Our older grandchildren discover the wonders of science and human relationships, but we often concentrate on their grades and treat their learning as simply their jobs as students, without taking the time to wonder with them.

With older children we can ask them what they have learned in their classes. As they reflect on their science classes we can wonder with them about the awe-inspiring parts of God's world. From their English classes we can marvel over our God-given ability to communicate and the beauty of words. From their physical education classes we can marvel over the way that God put us together and how our muscles respond to training.

There are simple references in the Bible that can be recalled as we wonder:

~ When we see the rain on the trees we can quote Psalm 147:8:

[God] fills the sky with clouds and sends rain to the earth,
so that the hills will be green with grass.

~ When we watch the ants carrying pieces of food larger than themselves we recall the proverb,

You lazy people can learn by watching an anthill.
Ants don't have leaders,
but they store up food during harvest season (Proverbs 6:6-8).

~ The tulips of the spring remind us of the words of Song of Songs 2:11-12:

Winter is past, the rain has stopped;
flowers cover the earth, it's time to sing.
The cooing of doves is heard in our land.

If we read the Bible with the desire to wonder, many more references that remind us of God's r the world and in our lives. Recognizing the wond our world need not be reserved for young children or for our grandchildren. Many adults need this reminder as we rush through our busy lives.

Reflect

~ What wonder of God's world did you miss today? yesterday? last week?
~ When can you make a point to share this wonder with your grandchildren?
~ With whom, besides grandchildren, can you share God's wonder?

Pray

Thank you, God, for all that you have given us in our world. Forgive us for passing by without stopping to wonder. Give us the pause that we need to put all of this awe-inspiring world into perspective. Amen.

Lessons of Rocks

Scripture: Anyone who hears and obeys these teachings of mine is like a wise person who built a house on solid rock. Rain poured down, rivers flooded, and winds beat against that house. But it did not fall, because it was built on solid rock.
                                                        —Matthew 7:24-25

My grandson, typical of many boys, went through a stage where he collected rocks. However, he went further than most boys in identifying the rocks and sorting them into categories.

When we visited in his home, he was kind enough to let us sleep in his room. As I looked through his rock collection, I was reminded of Jesus' parable about building a house on a rock instead of on shifting sand.

Jesus was a carpenter, and as a master craftsman he would have understood how foolish it is not to build on a solid rock foundation. During a recent trip to New York City I was fascinated by the skyline of the city. Tall buildings make up the skyline on both ends of Manhattan Island, and there are no tall buildings in the center. When I quizzed our guide, he told me that each end of the island has the deep, solid rock foundation needed for skyscrapers, but that solid bedrock is missing in the middle of the island.

This parable is one of several that Jesus told illustrating the difference between simply knowing what we should do and actually acting on those principles. We can easily learn the ethics of our religious teachings, but unless we dig deep into their meaning and apply our lives to the solid foundations, then we cannot stand firm when the storms of life sweep over us. Knowing something does not necessarily equate to doing it. But by our actions, we show the world that we know how to live a life of love.

My grandson's fascination with rocks keeps me alert to my need to be founded in the bedrock of our faith. To go a bit further in Jesus' illustration of building our faith on a firm foundation, we can recognize that our faith foundation can be set on a sturdy rock at one point, but unless we continue to dig down into that rock, the timbers of the faith can topple. When I begin to gloss over the important issues, or when I simply accept something because another person tells me, "It is so," then I find that my foundation is no longer strong. I must continually dig down into the solid foundation of Christ's teachings.

Reflect
~ What threatens the foundations of your faith? Are they real threats to the true foundations, or are they threats to the façade of the "building"?
~ What are some of the solid rock foundations of your faith?
~ How can you continue to dig into and question those foundations?

Pray
God, I want to establish my faith on your firm foundation. I will not only learn about your will, but I will work to carry out that will that you have for me. Amen.

Lessons of Excitement

**Scripture: It made me glad to hear them say,
 "Let's go to the house of the LORD!"**

—Psalm 122:1

When my grandchildren were young, every day was very much the same. They didn't understand the concept of time well enough to anticipate future days. But then when they heard their mother say, "This is the day we go to church!" their eyes lit up with excitement.

How wonderful to see that church ignites excitement for them! I should learn to step out of the routine and step into their type of enthusiasm. Those of us who have been in the church for a long time often become lulled into the "business as usual" mode. In fact, we come to expect the same "menu" as we go to worship. When there is a change, we even complain that it's not the same old same old. Even the newer styles of worship can become routine as they establish their own traditions. Following the same pattern can soon become monotonous.

We all grow spiritually in our own unique and personal ways. New research indicates that our personalities, rather than our age, determine the worship style that is most meaningful to us. Some of us seek out worship that is filled with liturgy and has its roots in our heritage. Some need a worship that is very high-energy. And there are those who need a more contemplative form of worship that centers on quiet music, scripture, and silence. When we know that we will grow spiritually through our worship, then we can be joyful with anticipation as we approach the church.

As my twin granddaughters skip down the walk leading to the church building, their excitement is obvious and contagious. I can tell the difference in my own attitude toward church when I'm with them. If they happen to be away or can't attend due to an illness, I find that my approach to the church becomes more matter-of-fact.

Reflect

~ What sort of signal does your smile and the spring in your step give to the people you meet as you come to church?

~ Do you recognize that in church we stand as we sing the opening song or hymn in the same manner that we would stand if a king were to enter the room, symbolizing that Christ is King?

~ Do you leave the church with excitement about ways you can take God into the community and keep God in every part of your daily life?

Pray

Help me learn from the children, Lord, that the church is a great place to be. Remind me that I am there to worship you and to prepare to serve. Amen.

Lessons of Sharing the Joy of Grandparenting

Scripture: About eight days later Jesus took Peter, John, and James with him and went up on a mountain to pray. While he was praying, his face changed, and his clothes became shining white. Suddenly Moses and Elijah were there speaking with him. They appeared in heavenly glory and talked about all that Jesus' death in Jerusalem would mean.

Peter and the other two disciples had been sound asleep. All at once they woke up and saw how glorious Jesus was. They also saw the two men who were with him.

Moses and Elijah were about to leave, when Peter said to Jesus, "Master, it is good for us to be here! Let us make three shelters, one for you, one for Moses, and one for Elijah." But Peter did not know what he was talking about.

While Peter was still speaking, a shadow from a cloud passed over them, and they were frightened as the cloud covered them. From the cloud a voice spoke, "This is my chosen Son. Listen to what he says!"

After the voice had spoken, Peter, John, and James saw only Jesus. For some time they kept quiet and did not say anything about what they had seen.

—Luke 9:28-36

When I first had grandchildren, I wanted to shout the joy to the world. This experience was so important to me that I wanted to share it with everyone. I was a typical grandma with pictures in her pocketbook. (I still carry pictures in my wallet, if you care to see them!)

But soon I realized that all the shouting in the world won't give others the same joy that I feel. They must experience that joy themselves. Then they will feel more excitement about their own experience than they ever could by hearing my stories. Their grandparenting experience is theirs, and mine is mine. The act of grandparenting becomes more sacred as I dwell on it myself instead of glibly talking about it constantly.

This is something like what happened to Peter, John, and James. Their mountaintop experience was great for them. They wanted to build temples to commemorate the occurrence. The temples, or houses, would have been for them, but they would also have been a way to testify to the world that they had had such a great experience. However, they heard the voice and kept quiet. We know the rest of the story from Acts. After a period of reflection they moved among the people, helping them recognize Christ and helping them have an experience with him themselves.

Experience is the basis of our spiritual growth. It is important for us to come into contact with God in many ways. Just as with grandparenting, we cannot bestow our own experience with God on other people. We can tell them about it, but they must have the experience themselves to truly appreciate it.

Reflect

~ When have you had an experience with God that you wanted to shout about to the world?

~ How can you help others experience God?

~ How can you help your grandchildren experience God?

Pray

My God, help me dwell on my experiences with you, but not in a boastful way. Help me realize that we each have our own ways of growing close to you, and mine may not be the same as another's, but that's okay. Give me appreciation for my experiences and the wisdom to allow others to experience you in their own way. Amen.

Lessons of Welcoming

Scripture: "When you welcome even a child because of me, you welcome me. And when you welcome me, you welcome the one who sent me."

—Mark 9:37

I had the honor of witnessing the baptism of all four of my grandchildren. Each baptism was a moment of excitement and joy. According to my recollection, baptisms during my childhood were not as special. The immediate family was there, but a baptism seldom involved the extended family. In fact, it was unusual for the siblings of the infant to stand up with the parents. This may simply have been the circumstances of where I lived. Today, however, we treat baptism with far greater importance. We excitedly share this action with our family and friends. With the experiences of these infant baptisms I have learned the lesson of welcoming.

No matter what your personal belief about infant baptism, all children should be welcomed into their religious family in some way. The little ones may not understand it, but those in the family of faith will recognize the children differently. The statement "It takes a village to raise a child" is even more important in our community of faith. Each one of us has a responsibility to contribute toward the faith development of every child.

Experiences and relationships are the primary impacts on the faith of both children and youth. First they experience happy times at church and joyful relationships with their care-givers. As their understanding develops, we plan specific times of worship. With experiential study they become more aware of our spiritual heritage and learn to seek God's guidance. Throughout this time we as adults in the church must take the initiative to affirm the child's personhood. This may be by simply learning the name of each child and using it. It may mean stooping down to their eye level and greeting them. It may mean providing adequate meeting areas for them throughout their childhood and youth years.

After we have welcomed them as children and during their beginning youth years, they have an opportunity to take the vows of membership on their own. Then we must welcome them as dedicated members of the faith. We accept them, even in their generational differences, because as Jesus said, if you accept one of these you accept him.

However, welcoming goes much further than simply accepting. To fully welcome someone you recognize their worth in the community, or in this case in the family of faith. Youth who have made the commitment of membership are full-fledged members. Their opinions on matters are impor-tant. They can take leadership responsibility, and without the opportunity to practice that leadership, they will not be pre-pared for the future of the church.

And so the lesson of welcoming is important not only with our grandchildren but with every child and youth in our churches.

Reflect

~ How can you help your grandchild remember his or her welcome into the church family?

~ What children or youth in your church family need your recognition, and how can you give it to them?

~ What young members of your church family need encouragement in leadership?

Pray

My God, help me welcome the children as Jesus modeled. Open my eyes to those who need my welcoming hugs and my inclusive smiles. Amen.

Lessons of Accomplishment

Scripture: Share your plans with the LORD, and you will succeed.

—Proverbs 16:3

When it comes to grades, my older grandchildren, who have been in school for a few years, can be proud. Of course, they have worked for good grades, but their work pays off.

Is pride, however, all there is to it? We learn that too much pride can cause a fall. Much depends on whether we are looking at the end product (the good grade) or whether we are looking for the joy of accomplishment, the joy of following God's leadership and accomplishing where we know God is leading us.

I can remember times in my own schooling when I truly felt a joy of accomplishing the assignment. It was an attitude that said, "Hey, I can do this!" I was not thinking about the grade I would receive, but I was thinking how much fun it was to really finish the task.

Sometimes today I miss that joy. I burden myself with so many projects and dreams of success that my only thought is to get to the end. I fail to appreciate the in-between joys of accomplishment. I see the project as one big assignment, when I could break it down into smaller units and find joy in the end product of each unit.

The old saying goes, "Rome was not built in a day." We have become too accustomed to instant potatoes, instant dinners, and even instant parties. We miss the joy of planning and the joy of preparation. We forget the smell of air-dried sheets as we fret about the time it takes to throw a load of wash into a dryer and to fold it afterwards. When the computer has a problem, we're ready to throw it out and get a new one. We forget how much we have accomplished just by having a computer instead of writing everything by hand. There is great joy along the way that we stumble over and either grumble about or ignore.

I can learn from my younger grandchildren, who delight in fitting a round peg into a round hole. My attitude is more like frantically trying to put together a thousand-piece puzzle just to see the end result. I miss the joy of finding the right puzzle piece a thousand times!

Reflect

~ What "instant" products do you take advantage of without appreciating them? How could you better use the time you save with these?

~ In what way are you pushing for accomplishment instead of enjoying the process or experience?

~ Where can you change your attitude and dwell on all that is around you?

Pray

Help me, Lord, to recognize the joy in accomplishment. Help me stop and appreciate the process as well as looking forward to the end product. Amen.

Lessons of Being Chosen

Scripture: The Lord has given us this command,
*   "I have placed you here as a light for the Gentiles.*
*   You are to take the saving power of God*
*   to people everywhere on earth."*

—Acts 13:47

I need someone to do something for me. Whom shall I choose?" I asked.

"Choose me! Choose me!" Such a clamor of voices! Young grandchildren always want to be the one chosen, even if they don't know what they're chosen for. Older grandchildren are a little more cautious, recognizing that they may not want to do the request that I have.

God did not ask the Hebrew people if they wanted to carry out the mission. God said, "I choose you!" (See Isaiah 43:10) But the Hebrew people did not always understand that they were chosen to be God's servants and take the message to others.

There is a classic book called *Hope for the Flowers*, by Trina Paulus. It's the story of two caterpillars, Yellow and Stripe, who are very good friends. They discover a pile of caterpillars and begin climbing the pile to find out what is at the top. In their climb they not only step all over other caterpillars but eventually they step on each other.

Yellow gives up the climb and meets another caterpillar, who is spinning hairy stuff all over himself. As the other caterpillar spins, he explains to Yellow that she doesn't need to climb to the top of the pile, because there is a butterfly within herself, which is what she is meant to be. But in order to become a butterfly, she must give up being a caterpillar. Meanwhile, Stripe reaches the top to find that there is nothing there, only other caterpillars struggling to stay on top. When Yellow finally becomes a butterfly, she flies to the top of the pile; and Stripe comes down the pile and eventually discovers the butterfly within himself.

We clamor to be the chosen one. We enjoy being the "top dog" in any situation. But God has chosen us to move out of our current existence and share the message with all people. God's choosing of us is not to be the "top dog" above others but to be servants.

It's really uncertain at times just what God is asking us to do. And that makes us a bit fearful. If we follow God's direction, we may have to give up life as we know it. We may have inconveniences, or we may lose some friends. But unless we find the calling that is within us, we will never grow our wings and fly.

My young grandchildren shout, "Choose me! Choose me!" because they love me. I must learn to answer God's call for the same reason, because I love God.

Reflect
~ What is God calling you to do?
~ What sort of inconvenience will this cause for you?
~ Do you love God enough to put up with these inconveniences? How can you open yourself more fully to God's will in your life?

Pray
My God, I hear your call. Sometimes it isn't completely clear as to the specifics. But I know that my love must be so strong that I will follow your call, no matter what. Amen.

Lessons of Words and Seeds

Scripture: "Rain and snow fall from the sky.
But they don't return without watering the earth
*   that produces seeds to plant and grain to eat.*
That's how it is with my words.

*They don't return to me without doing everything
I send them to do."*

—*Isaiah 55:10-11*

It was a venture in gardening. I remembered how my older grandchildren loved the garden that their father helped them plant and tend, and so we set up a small garden plot for our younger granddaughters. The first year their memory was short, and the act of planting the carrots was forgotten by the time they came to harvest. But the girls did enjoy pulling the carrots up and having them for the evening meal.

The next year I was smart enough to plant peas that produced in a shorter time. The girls even helped me water the garden from time to time, and they saw the progress of the growth. When the peas were ready, the girls enjoyed them even more as we ate them in the garden than they did when the peas were cooked and on their plates.

As we talked of how God sent the rain to water the seeds and make them grow, I was reminded of the verses from Isaiah. As three-year-olds, my granddaughters were not into abstract thinking enough to understand the correlation between the rain and God's words, but their experience with planting brought the scripture words to my mind.

I thought about God's words and how much I appreciate those words in the Bible that gave me guidance and wisdom. I've often said that God did not give me the gift of memory, and so it is difficult if not impossible for me to memorize anything word-for-word perfect. But I do recall many, many scriptures. I remember their context and their meanings. I remember the rhythm of the words. I remember that they go deep inside me when I read them. Then I turn to the Bible that I have used for many years, having underlined so many of the verses. Those verses jump out at me as I thumb through the pages. This is my way of living with the Word when I cannot memorize.

And truly, I am sure that God's words are like rain, causing my faith to grow and not returning to God until they have accomplished what they were set forth to do. I hope that my grandchildren will someday recognize just what God's words can do for them too. I will tell them how experiences with God's words have helped me grow in my faith.

Reflect
~ What words of God are most meaningful to you? How do you keep those words before you?
~ How have you grown in your understanding of God's Word?
~ How can you pass these important words on to children as they grow?

Pray
My God, I do thank you for the words that guide me. May I be like seeds in fertile ground, allowing the rain of your words to soak into the earth around me and nourish me. Amen.

Lessons of the Moment

Scripture: God said, "Now we will make humans, and they will be like us. We will let them rule the fish, the birds, and all other living creatures."

—*Genesis 1:26*

I began a journal for our twin granddaughters, whom I frequently babysit. The journal began simply as recording my thoughts about my time with these girls, but as I realized that their mother was not able to experience some of their "firsts," it expanded to recording many of the things that they did as they grew. I decided also to include some pictures of these memories.

Then came the problem. Each time I tried to get good pictures of specific actions, the girls foiled me and refused to carry out the action, or they did it in a manner that did not offer an opportunity for me to get a good shot. I found that I needed to have my camera ready at all times and take the picture when the action happened naturally. I could not force it upon them.

The twins taught me that I needed to be prepared to seize the moment! They showed me that God did certainly create us as individuals. Being created in God's image gives us free will, the ability to have a mind of our own. There are times when we think that we must bow to other people's desires, and sometimes it is necessary in order to live peacefully with others. But we do that of our own choice. This is a part of God's will.

Leslie Weatherhead, a British pastor during World War II, gave a series of sermons that have since been published in a book, *The Will of God.* (Abingdon Press: Nashville, 1972). He shares his understanding that God's will is threefold, distinguishing something as being "within God's will" instead of simply being God's will:

God's Original Will—We are created in God's image, to live a happy life loving each other. However, as an image of God we are given our own individual will, and we can choose our actions. We are not puppets on a string.

God's Circumstantial Will—Sometimes we choose to do things that are harmful to others, or sometimes we have not grown in our knowledge enough to know how to deal with the circumstances of nature or of illness. Those circumstances are within God's will simply because God created us with a will of our own. These are the times that God "weeps" with us.

God's Ultimate Will—If we look to God in all circumstances, we will grow even in the harsh times of our lives. Because of these, God's ultimate will comes through, and we are stronger and better individuals from the experiences.

Reflect
~ When have you seen God's circumstantial will and felt that God was weeping with you?
~ How have you grown stronger because you lived through certain circumstances?
~ How can you seize the moment and find God in every situation?

Pray
Thank you, God, for being with me even in the times I didn't realize your nearness. Give me the understanding of all that you allow within your will. Amen.

Lessons of Prayer

Scripture: Always be joyful and never sto
—1 Thes ...unans 5:16-17

We were at a restaurant with a large group of people. We had waited for some time for our food, and when it arrived we continued to visit together as we ate. My grandchild, who was sitting next to me, interrupted my conversation with a pat on my arm, "Gran, we forgot to pray."

I needed to respect that interruption. We were certainly being joyful, but we certainly weren't praying. Although we were in a public place, I learned to remember our routine of prayer before eating, and again a child did lead us.

Jesus seemed to always recognize that God was with him. I often tell parents that prayer does not require a specific posture of the body, or even closing our eyes. Why do we bow our heads and close our eyes to pray? We bow our heads to indicate humbleness to God. The word *humble* comes from the same root word as *humus*. We speak of humus when we compost vegetation and then use it as soil to grow food. When we humble ourselves before God, we symbolically become as humus, offering ourselves to be used by God.

We close our eyes to shut out distractions. For very young children, closing their eyes is unnatural, unless they are in

...eep; and they certainly don't understand the concept ...bleness. Children will imitate us by bowing their heads ...d closing their eyes. But we need not insist that such action is necessary to pray. When I am a passenger in a car, I certainly hope that the driver will not close his or her eyes to pray when we encounter a stressful situation.

We need to be comfortable praying in any circumstance. I often lead people in "open-eyed prayer." I will ask them to look around the room at the faces of those with them, and we pray our thanks for the occasion. When I see a lovely sunset, instead of saying, "Look at the lovely sunset," I say, "I thank God for the lovely sunset!" Although the sentence does not begin with "Dear God," it is certainly a form of prayer. We can enjoy the tempting sights and smells of a meal before us and thank God for it. We can use our eyes to savor the smiles of friends as we pray our thanks to God.

Living with prayer happens in a natural way when we remain conscious of the many opportunities to share God with our grandchildren. We lead children in experiences now that they will label later.

Reflect
~ What opportunity to pray an open-eyed prayer have you missed recently?
~ When can you share an open-eyed prayer with a child?
~ How is your attitude of humbleness reflected in your actions?

Pray

My God, I recognize that prayer is a conversation with you. Help me be in continuous conversation as I live in the joy of your love. Amen.

Lessons of the Moon

Scripture: You created the moon to tell us the seasons. The sun knows when to set.

—Psalm 104:19

Each morning when my twin granddaughters were young and arrived for their day with me, their mother and I lifted them out of their car seats into the darkness of the dawn. The first thing they did was look up into the sky, searching for the moon. When they saw it, there were squeals of recognition. There it was, just as they knew it would be, hanging in the sky!

I learn to see God through the excited eyes of little ones. I see the moon and appreciate its brightness, its change in form, its coming and going, its mystery and its charm.

As my granddaughters grow older, I will help them see how God set the earth in a cycle, with the moon rising at different times during the month. We will talk about how the moon sets the seasons. This will be science, yes, but it will be science with a foundation. God will be at the source of the seasons, even as the seasons change. Then my appreciation for our dependable God will be strengthened. I will see God again with new eyes.

Mystery is part of the whole world. Mystery is at the heart of religion. If we knew all there is to know about God, then God would not be God. When the writers of the book of Genesis delved into the mystery of our existence and the existence of all that is around us, they came upon the genuine truth that God is at the source of our being, no matter how it came about.

But the truth was, and still is, embedded in mystery. The explanation that the early writers used for mystery grew as they searched to understand God. It was a developing comprehension of our beginnings. With each generation we peel away the layers of the mystery of life, and with each layer we grow closer to the heart of the great mystery that is truth. We draw closer to the greatness of God and to the way God created our world, as it interacts with all facets of creation.

When I look up at the moon and hear my grandchild say, "Ahhh! Moon!" I know for sure that there is a God. I cannot explain it, but I know it to be true.

Reflect

~ What early concepts of God do you recall as a child?

~ How have those concepts changed?

~ When has the moon brought thoughts of God to your mind?

Pray

My Creator, God, I marvel at your creation. Thank you for the dependability of the moon and for the mystery that is a part of your world. Help me bask in that mystery, even as I learn a little more about you from children. Amen.

Lessons of Names

Scripture: I promise that you will be the father of many nations. That's why I now change your name from Abram to Abraham. I will give you a lot of descendants, and in the future they will become great nations. Some of them will even be kings.
—*Genesis 17:4-6*

What's in a name? Does it matter what we are called? Does a name make a difference in the personality, or does a personality set the attitude toward a name?

My first two grandchildren call me *Grandma*. I liked the name *Nana*, but their other grandmother asked for it first, and I've been very happy with *Grandma*. It's what I called my grandmothers, and it's what my children called my mother.

When our daughter adopted her twins, we talked about what they would call me. I said I wasn't particular, but I'd prefer that it not be *Granny*. That name sent up images of Granny from *The Beverly Hillbillies*, and that was not the image I wanted to portray. *Grandma* seemed a long handle, so we shortened it to *Gran*. At age two, the twins came up with their own idea. Wouldn't you know, they called me *Granny*, as plain as can be. Well, I've decided that instead of taking on *The Beverly Hillbillies* image, I'll change the image of the name! I'll be a much more modern Granny, but I'll still be the loving grandmother I've tried to be for my older grandchildren.

We read in the Bible how God changed the names of Abram and Sarai to Abraham and Sarah. Although these older people were anxious for a son, they may have been concerned about the interruption in their routine that a baby would bring. We read about Sarah laughing over the situation, and I imagine it was a nervous laugh. I'm sure that Abraham and Sarah felt they were leaving their old life behind and beginning a new chapter with new names. They were now embarking on the role of parenthood, not just parenthood of a son, but of a whole new nation. And that nation would have a responsibility in forming a deeper understanding of God. What an awesome responsibility! What an awesome honor!

It's not necessary for us to have new names in order to begin a new adventure of God. It only takes a discovery of where God is leading us and a determination to follow. But how do we know the direction God wants us to go? I can't tell you just how to know the direction, but I can say that it will certainly be in keeping with your gifts and talents. Those talents may be lying dormant for a while, or you may not even have discovered them yet, but I don't believe God demands that we work in an area without giving us the tools with which to work. Sometimes they just need a little sharpening.

When we consider what's in a name, we can either take on the image of the name or we can launch a new image for the name we have, using the talents God gave us. In any case, it is important to make that image in keeping with God's will for our lives.

Reflect

~ How are you living out your name? Even if you don't know what your name means, what image are you giving to your name for others to see?

~ In what direction do you feel God wants you to go now?

~ How can you help children recognize that God has a plan for their lives?

Pray

God of Abraham, give me the view of just what you want me to do for you. Help me realize that you can interrupt the routine and point me in a new direction. Give me the courage to follow. Amen.

Lessons of Differences

**Scripture: You are the one who put me together
 inside my mother's body,
and I praise you
 because of the wonderful way you created me.
Everything you do is marvelous!
 Of this I have no doubt.**

—Psalm 139:13-14

Before our daughter adopted twin girls, I had had very little experience with twins. I have cousins who are twins, but I lived a distance from them and saw them only about once a year as I was growing up. They were no more alike than any two sisters. In fact, they were very different. They were fraternal twins. In recent years I've learned new terms for twins: dizygotic (twins from two eggs, fertilized by separate sperm) and monozygotic (twins from one fertilized egg that splits into two embryos). This takes away the understanding that "identical" twins must be identical.

My granddaughters are mono(one)-zygotic(egg) twins, and although to most people they look identical, there is a definite difference in their interests, and it appears there will be a difference in their gifts or talents. No matter that they came from the same egg and probably have the same DNA, God has made each twin an individual. Both girls love music, which is typical of their South Pacific birth heritage. One girl, however, seems to have a greater desire for music, and the other is more athletically inclined. One twin is more adventuresome than the other, yet they both love to cuddle in your arms. And all of this may change as the years progress.

I find it amazing that God has made each of us different in our own way. Each of us is an individual, not to be duplicated through the natural genetic process. Each individual is his or her own person.

The problem comes when we try to make other people fit into our molds. We think that our way is the only way of doing things, or we think that everyone should want to dress or style their hair in the same manner as we do. Then we look down on those who do not conform. We ridicule them in an effort to build ourselves up and make ourselves superior to them.

My twin granddaughters have taught me that it is good to be my own person. It is good to stand up for what I believe, even if it isn't what people around me believe. It is good to be a part of the great, diverse world that God made.

The psalmist told it as it is. He wrote about our differentness, and he affirmed it, recognizing that God planned and made it that way. What an awesome God we worship! What a great way to give us refreshment and to give us many ways of seeing God and of seeing God's world.

Reflect

~ How are you different from the other people in your church? in your family? in your life? Do you affirm that differentness?

~ Do you listen to people who have different religious ideas from yours? Do you listen with an open heart?

~ How can you use your individualism to affirm the special characteristics of others?

Pray

Dear God, thank you for the creativeness of your world. Give me eyes to see each and every person from your point of view. Help me affirm the uniqueness of others. Amen.

Lessons of Dreams

Scripture: Jesus and his disciples went to the villages near the town of Caesarea Philippi. As they were walking along, he asked them, "What do people say about me?"

The disciples answered, "Some say you are John the Baptist or maybe Elijah. Others say you are one of the prophets."

Then Jesus asked them, "But who do you say I am?"

"You are the Messiah!" Peter replied.

—Mark 8:27-29

Before I had grandchildren I dreamed of the times I would hold the babies in my arms, whispering my love in their ears and feeling their soft skin on my face. There were dreams of moments we would share exploring God's world, and times when I would burst with pride at one of their concerts or sporting events.

But babies, even grandchildren, come with their own agendas. They get hungry and cry for food. They mess in their diapers and must be changed. As they grow older, they stubbornly refuse to do what you want them to do, or they whine about things, grating on your nerves. They eventually choose their friends' company over that of their grandparents.

The Hebrew people dreamed of a Messiah who would take over the world politically and place them at the top again, as they had been when David was their king. When the Messiah came, things were not as they had expected. Jesus was born in humble surroundings. He gathered an assortment of people to be the followers whom he could train and entrust with his mission. He even opposed the accepted religious leaders of his day. What kind of Messiah was this? It was certainly not the Messiah of their dreams!

When we dream, our anticipation shapes the dream as we like it. We spin all sorts of ideas of just how we want things to be. That's why we call them dreams, I guess. These thoughts are not real. They often don't even contain a thread of reality. They're "pie in the sky by and by" type dreams.

But then, reality sets in. Life is not always what we dream it to be. The Messiah may become more demanding, requiring us to take action instead of just sitting back and watching the Messiah do it all. In reality, we may not want the dream of a Messiah to come about, because it is not as we dreamed it. The reality takes dedication and backbone.

Just as the dream of grandchildren doesn't always turn out as we expected, our Christian journey is harder than any dream we ever had. But it is a joyful hardship!

Reflect
~ How is life different for you from what you expected as a beginning Christian?
~ Who has helped you see the reality of Christianity?
~ How does God help you cope with the reality?

Pray
Your dream is sometimes different from mine, God. But I know that you can pull me through any hard time in the reality of life. I count on that! Amen.

Lessons of Solitude

**Scripture: But I have calmed and quieted my soul,
like a weaned child with its mother;
my soul is like the weaned child that is with me.**
—Psalm 131:2 (NRSV)

I often observe one of my grandchildren simply sitting or standing and looking at nothing in particular. What, I wonder, is going through the child's mind? With the older children I could ask such a question, but I'm not sure I want to. Their gazing into the world may be a search for solitude, a time to search within themselves. I would not want to disturb that special time with God, as they understand God.

Adults have the capability of going apart from others and finding a place for solitude, but children cannot do that. And so children sometimes shut out the world and seek solitude within. But, even though we have the capability, do we adults go apart for solitude? What holds us back? Do we feel somehow that seeking solitude is a demeaning action? Do we fear being labeled undignified or inadequate?

Think about the phrase "being alone." What concepts does that phrase bring to mind? Rejection? Unpopularity? Being left out? These words reflect society's concept of the phrase. They reflect isolation rather than solitude. In isolation we are cut off from others involuntarily, whereas solitude is a choice. We enter solitude with a different frame of mind. We can be forced into isolation, but no one can force us into solitude. This is the way of a healthy relationship with God, by choice. God never forces us into relationship, but rather welcomes us when we come of our own volition. Time alone with God, then, is solitude.

The psalmist brings to our minds the difference between a nursing child searching for food, and a child who calmly sits with the mother, not begging and demanding, but appreciating the love that the mother's arms bestow. Perhaps we can compare this to the way that we pray to God. Instead of a begging or demanding prayer, we should find times to approach God in peaceful solitude. Prayer can be simply opening our hearts and accepting God's love. There are times when we may need to hash things over with God, and that's okay. The psalmists certainly give us examples of that too. But we must always set aside times simply to be with God and to bask in the love called "grace."

Reflect
~ When have you set aside time to spend alone with God?
~ What blocks your commitment to solitude? How can you get around that block?
~ How can you help your grandchildren (or friends who are children) appreciate solitude?

Pray
Lord, I hear you calling me to come apart and spend time in solitude with you. Give me the courage to push aside all that hounds my time and dedicate some time for you. Amen.

Lessons from the Seasons

Scripture: Everything on earth has its own time and its own season.... Yet none of us can ever fully understand all [God] has done, and [God] puts questions in our minds about the past and the future.

—Ecclesiastes 3:1, 11

I grew up in Florida, where many people say there is only one season. However, on closer observation you will realize that Florida has many more seasons than most locations; they are just more subtle. There is the season of orange blossoms, and the season of the citrus fruit. There is the season of migrating birds, and the mating season of the alligator. Whether we live in a tropical climate or a climate of drastic seasonal change, we can recognize the nature cycles that God placed in the world. One of my favorite answers to my grandchildren's questions is, "God made it that way!" And it is so.

In the fall I walk with my grandchildren through the leaves, scuffing them along with my feet. We listen to the crunch as the brittle leaf fibers break with each step. Then I thank God for ears to hear. As I hear the leaves, I also hear the delightful voices of the grandchildren, "Look, Grandma! Here is a red one!"

Then we look at the brilliant scarlet color and remember that God made the colors. God could have made the world in black-and-white, and we'd never have known the difference. What a gift God has given us with color! And in the spring and summer we again see color in the plants, knowing that our dependable God has seen us through a cycle and we can enjoy the color once again.

On a rainy day I tell my grandchildren that God recycles the water in our world. The water is drawn up into the sky and is released again to fall to the earth. We sometimes interrupt the cycle, and this can cause problems. For example, we cut down the rainforests or we put too many pollutants in the air. I am reminded that we must respect the systems within God's plan.

What a joy it is to see the seasons of God's world through the eyes of grandchildren. They are learning about change and progression. They are learning that God is dependable. God has set in motion the cycles, and we can depend on them coming again next year. Through my grandchildren's learning, I renew my joy in God. As I see the wonder in their eyes, I again wonder at our great God. Without them to remind me, I might become numb to all that is around me.

Reflect

~ What cycles do you often overlook in the world around you? How can you point them out to children?

~ How does the phrase "God made it that way" answer unanswerable questions for you?

~ What do you see in the world this day that makes you realize that God is a mystery?

Pray

God of the seasons, help me renew my joy in you each time I experience a change in your world. Send me children who will point your way to me again and again and again. Amen.

Lessons of New Things

Scripture: I am creating something new. There it is! Do you see it?
I have put roads in deserts, streams in thirsty lands.
—Isaiah 43:19

Where did that idea come from? I ask myself this question often when I'm with my grandchildren. It seems that every time I see them, there is a new thought process or a new physical achievement.

Yesterday they couldn't complete a somersault, and today they're flipping across the floor.

It's been weeks since we blew bubbles through a small wand, and today they improvise with the latch for the dog's leash, pretending that it is the wand and trying to blow bubbles through it with water.

For months they held on to the wall while coming down the stairs, and today they walk down and don't even seem to realize that they are not holding on.

It seems like only yesterday when my granddaughter simply hit the piano keys, and now I have received a video of her playing "When the Saints Go Marching In" at a piano recital.

And when did my young grandson become a young man who enjoys adult conversations?

Look! Do you see? God is creating something new! As I watch my grandchildren grow and change, I realize that God continually creates. Every day is a new day with a newness to God's creation. Every day there is something more to marvel over, if only I watch for it. Every day the growth and development of my grandchildren draw me closer to God.

How do I miss the newness of God's creation? Do I see it in a new sunrise? Do I see it in the baby birds that come to my feeder? Do I see it in a new relationship with a neighbor?

And how am I instrumental in helping that new creation

come about? Am I conscious of the environment and the ways that my actions affect the change in my surroundings? Do I allow God's creativity to work through me and bring about new solutions to old problems?

Reflect
~ What new thing have you seen today?
~ Where are you blocking God's creation of a new thing?
~ How can you thank and praise God for each new creation?

Pray
My God, how wondrous is life with you! How exciting to see something new come about in your world and in your people! Give me the observation abilities to recognize the new thing when I see it, and the opportunities to share the newness with others. Amen.

Lessons from Communion

Scripture: When the time came for Jesus and the apostles to eat, he said to them, "I have very much wanted to eat this Passover meal with you before I suffer."

—Luke 22:14-15

It seemed to be a routine Communion service. Sometimes the service becomes *too* routine, and we miss the real meaning. I have always felt that it is important for children to feel they are a part of the family of God, and what better way than to enjoy the special meal that we call Communion or the Lord's Supper. They may not understand the full meaning of the occasion (and who of us adults really understands it?), but they know that it is a special time for all of God's children.

On this particular occasion, no adult was guiding my young granddaughter's hand. She received the wafer from the Communion server and moved to the person holding the cup. She had seen others dip the wafer into the cup, and she did the same. But in her enthusiasm she dipped her whole hand into the cup. Fortunately the server simply smiled and wiped her hand with a towel after she had eaten the wafer.

As I reflected on what others may consider a mistake, I realized how symbolic this experience was—how out of the routine. We must all totally immerse ourselves in the experience of Christ to receive God's love. Without the total giving-over of our lives as Christ gave his life, we cannot experience the fullness of God's love. We dwell in the surface love, dipping into the sacrament (or holy moment) only briefly.

Now, each time I go forward to receive the sacrament of Communion, I remember the lesson my granddaughter taught me. I try to give myself totally to the holy moment. I will never understand such a moment completely, but I realize that the mystery of the experience is a part of the holiness that surrounds me.

Reflect

~ What thoughts did you have when you last received Communion?

~ How can you make the sacrament a more holy moment in your life?

~ How can you share your understanding of the sacrament with a child?

Pray

God of the sacrament, direct my hand, but allow me to become totally immersed in your love. Bring me, as a child, to these holy moments, open and willing. Amen.

Lessons of Interruptions

Scripture: About that time Emperor Augustus gave orders for the names of all the people to be listed in record books. These first records were made when Quirinius was governor of Syria.

Everyone had to go to their own hometown to be listed. So Joseph had to leave Nazareth in Galilee and go to Bethlehem in Judea.

—Luke 2:1-4

Grandchildren can make quite a change in your life. Even when you do not live near the grandchildren, they can make an impact on your lifestyle, interrupting your routine. Suddenly you see baby clothes and cuddly toys in a different light. Or you dream of tossing a football with your grandson in the near future, even when the boy is not even able to sit up, let alone run for a ball. Most grandparents become GWPIPs (Grandparent With Pictures In Pocket/Purse). Jesus' birth must have made a difference in the life of his grandparents too, if they were still living at the time. Would they have seen the interruption as a blessing or a problem?

We were excited when we were expecting our first grandchild. We had a trip all mapped out. I had a women's retreat to lead in Kansas City, and we planned to drive back to Atlanta in time for the birth date! But our grandson surprised us and came early. We celebrated the occasion with our friends in Kansas City, left a little earlier than expected, and headed for Atlanta. Such excitement over a few pounds of human flesh! But this little man was more than that. As his father, our son, said, Jesse was to teach us more about God's love than anyone else could. Even before he learned to talk and before he learned to say "please" and "thank you," that baby taught us that God loves with unconditional love. We loved him just because he was a part of our family.

With the birth of this special child we recognized that if God's love for us is anything like our love for this first grandchild, then we could all come closer to understanding the word *grace*. We now saw that God can love us no matter what. We saw that God loves us simply because we belong to God. We are loved whether we use the many talents that God has given us or not. God loves us whether we are kind to others or not. God simply loves.

As the months went by, however, we learned another thing about love. As Jesse went through the process of returning our love, we recognized that we must return God's love and grow in our ability to love others.

Yes, that little man taught us much in his first years. And as our other grandchildren came along, we renewed that lesson. God's love is unconditional.

Reflect

~ Where have you experienced unconditional love?

~ When have you felt love for someone even amid disappointment?

~ How does that love correspond to God's love for you?

Pray

God of Grace, we recognize your love for us. We know that the event of Christ's birth interrupted the routine of many people in the world of that first century. We recognize that as a positive interruption. Give us the understanding of your love. Amen.

Lessons of Worship

Scripture: Sing a new song to the LORD!
Everyone on this earth, sing praises to the LORD.
—Psalm 96:1

It has amazed me how my grandchildren have adjusted to various forms of worship. I grew up in an era when we had only one form of worship in our denomination. Granted, sometimes we would attend another denomination and the worship service might not have instrumental music, or it might have incense, or more or less congregational singing. But as long as we attended a church of our denomination, we usually followed the same basic form of worship.

Now we recognize that different people grow spiritually by worshipping in different ways. In fact there is some research that indicates our personality has much to do with the way that we best grow spiritually. (Malcolm Goldsmith, *Knowing Me, Knowing God* [Abingdon Press: Nashville, 1997]) Many churches now plan several types of worship services so that each person can find that which fills his or her need. Some of us grow closer to God through liturgy. Others need a high-energy service. And still others find their souls reach out to God best through a contemplative service with periods of silence.

When the different forms of worship began to take shape in our churches, those of us who grew up with only one way to worship resisted the change. We had trouble accepting anything new! Was it the newness, or was it that the new way was not what drew us closer to God?

When I had a heart-to-heart conversation with someone who truly enjoyed the high-energy style of worship, I came to realize that she was sincere in her appreciation of this new worship, and she was not a young person. This actually touched her soul where it had never been touched before through liturgical worship. It awakened something in her that had lain dormant for many years. Worship had a new meaning for her! I then praised God for change, and I praised God that we can worship in ways that are best for each of us.

I cannot tell yet just what type of worship my grandchildren will find meets their individual needs, but I am happy that they will have a choice. Seeing them comfortable in different styles of worship helps me realize that they are growing in their faith. As their personalities develop they will find that which touches their souls and draws them closer to God. They will appreciate the importance of worship to each of us because they have experienced several ways to worship.

Reflect

~ What in your personality makes a certain type of worship more meaningful to you?
~ Have you experienced a new way of worship that has more meaning to you?
~ Whom can you talk to with an open mind who worships in a different way from you? What can you learn from them?

Pray

Our God, help me remember that worship can take many different forms. Jesus gave us a model for prayer, but he did not give us a spe-cific method for worship. Thank you, God, for the freedom to worship you in the way that draws me closest to you. Amen.

Lessons of Inquisitiveness

Scripture: You said to me, "I will point out the road that you should follow.
I will be your teacher and watch over you."

—Psalm 32:8

There is so much for children to learn, and they are so ready to learn it! From the time our grandchildren were able to follow movement with their eyes I witnessed a real inquisitiveness in them. First they would look at something new with an expression of delight or inquiry. Then they began moving their heads to follow any noise, as if to say, "What is that? What can I understand about it?"

I remember the games of hiding a toy or some other object behind my back or under my leg, and the grandchild reaching for my arm, trying to bring it out into the open. Then there were the games that delighted them where I would put something in my pocket, and they would push their little hands into my pocket just to see what I had.

When they were older, we played games of searching for something hidden in the room, and soon they were enjoying games as we rode in the car where I would mention something we were passing, and they would look quickly to see who could find it first.

Christmas and birthdays became a delight as they tore open packages and poked around in the paper stuffed into the boxes to see just what was hidden there. Indeed, often they enjoyed the paper more than the gift!

The older grandchildren soon became inquisitive about animals and plants, and about how the caterpillar changed into a butterfly or the tadpole became a frog. Our grandson pored over books of dinosaurs, curious about these creatures that lived long ago and are now extinct.

Through my grandchildren's eyes I am renewing my own sense of inquisitiveness. I want to know more about the world.

I want to understand how God acts in the world. I want to know more about the people of the Bible and how they grew in their understanding of God. I want to know more about how I can relate to God and learn to follow God's way for me. I want to know just what God will teach me and how God will watch over me. And I want to recognize and carry out my part in making the kingdom of God a real force in the world today. I am not too old for that! We are never too old to learn more about God and to follow God's direction in our lives.

Reflect
~ What have you seen through a child's inquisitiveness that you took for granted before?
~ What do you want to know about God that you hesitated to ask before? With whom can you talk about this?
~ Where in your life do you see God teaching and directing you today?

Pray
God of mystery, give me the curiosity to explore you in ways that I have never dared to do before. Show me your path and teach me your ways. Amen.

LESSONS OF CARING AND CONCERN

Lessons of Love

Scripture: Listen, Israel! The LORD our God is the only true God! So love the LORD your God with all your heart, soul, and strength.

—Deuteronomy 6:4-5

I had not seen our grandchildren in some time, and suddenly they were there, spilling out of the car and rushing to me. They threw their arms around my legs, calling my name over and over again. I knew that they loved me, even without their saying the words. How can you not see such love?

This made me wonder how I show others that I love God with my whole heart, soul, and strength. God is not in human form. I can't throw my arms around God with hugs and kisses. A Sunday-school lesson we recently had in our adult class suggested that the first commandment is the most important commandment of all, "Do not worship any god except me" (Deuteronomy 5:7). We worship that which we love the most. But how do I demonstrate this love?

Showing this love for God is what we call worship. This we do on Sunday morning in our time together as a family of God. But isn't worship something that should happen throughout the week? If worshiping God is showing our love for God, then does it only happen with singing and listening to a sermon? Perhaps I should learn from my grandchildren that loving happens 24/7. I can love and worship God as I care for the environment. I can love and worship God as I help a grandchild understand the cycles of growth in God's world. I can love and worship God as I prepare a meal or mow a lawn for a neighbor who is sick. I can love and worship God as I participate in a mission project or simply as I smile at a stranger who seems to need a bright spot in the day.

Where did we get the idea that worshiping God is done only in a certain ritual and with certain types of songs or prayers? Where did we get the idea that we worship God only at a certain place and a certain time? If we are to love and worship God with our whole heart, soul, and strength, then it will involve a rake and a cooking pot; a child's storybook, and a brush and paints; a computer program and a mechanic's wrench; a stethoscope and a garden hoe.

Worshiping God and loving God happens when we show love to others as well as when we raise our voices in praise and empty our souls in prayer. Worshiping God should become our whole goal in life and be lived out in every minute of every day.

That's how I love my grandchildren and how they love me. And that's how I hope to show my love for my God.

Reflect

~ How do you show your love for your grandchild or some other child who means the world to you?

~ What act have you done this day that reflects your love for God?

~ How can you remind yourself that your actions are a form of worship?

Pray

You ask us to love you, our God. Forgive me for limiting my worship to one hour on Sunday, and sometimes missing that time. Help me remember that loving you is a 24/7 undertaking and that I can do that with joy. Amen.

Lessons from Tears

Scripture: You, LORD, are my shepherd. I will never be in need.
   You let me rest in fields of green grass.
You lead me to streams of peaceful water,
   and you refresh my life.

You are true to your name,
   and you lead me along the right paths.
I may walk through valleys as dark as death,
   but I won't be afraid.
You are with me,
   and your shepherd's rod makes me feel safe.

You treat me to a feast, while my enemies watch.

You honor me as your guest,
  and you fill my cup until it overflows.

Your kindness and love will always be with me
each day of my life,
  and I will live forever in your house, LORD.

—Psalm 23

I had not seen our two-year-old twin granddaughters for several weeks when they came into our home. They surprised me by clinging to their mother. Tears rose in the eyes of one of the girls. She must have realized that she was to be left in my care.

I longed for things to be as they had been before our separation. Then they had run happily into my arms the minute they hit the door. I longed for them to see me as one who cares and who shields them from the pains and cruelty of the world. Perhaps I felt a bit like God does when we hesitate to accept the caring love that is available.

The psalmist expressed that loving attitude of God in a way that the biblical people could understand, because they knew of shepherds and their sheep. James Taylor, in his book *Everyday Psalms*, suggests that the metaphor of a mother could be used in today's world. Since we know so little about sheep, I'd suggest that a grandparent might be used to interpret the caring concern of God.

Lord, you are like a grandma to me.

You open your arms to me and fold me to your breast.

When I've been hurt you refresh me with your cool hand on my forehead, and I rest in your arms until I have courage.

When we go for walks, you help me watch for the cars.
I know that wherever we go you will be there to guide me,
    so I'm not afraid.
When I come into your house from a hot day of play or a
    hard day at school,
    you are there with a cookie and a cool glass of milk.
You know the kind of cookies I like best.
I'd like to have your gifts of love forever.
I know that even when I grow old, I will remember your
    house as special and your arms as love.

Reflect

~ How have you rejected God's care and guidance?
~ How have you seen God's care come to you through another
    person?
~ To whom might you offer God's love as the psalmist saw
    God's love in a shepherd?

Pray

*Our God and Grandparent, thank you for being there when we need
you. Thank you for the cool hand, and the cookies and milk of love.
Amen.*

Lessons of Listening

Scripture: You are my God and protector. Please answer my prayer.

I was in terrible distress, but you set me free.
  Now have pity and listen as I pray.

—*Psalm 4:1*

I must admit that there have been times when I've been so engrossed in something I was doing or reading that I've not immediately responded when a grandchild called my name. I suddenly realize that the child has called me, over and over again, trying to get my attention. I'm sure the child wonders if I'll ever answer, but continues to call.

Perhaps this is how David felt when he wrote the fourth psalm. As close as David was to God, his psalms sometimes indicate that he felt he was not receiving an answer.

But God is not like humans. God is always there, listening. If we feel that God is not answering, perhaps we actually are not tuned in to God's answer. Or perhaps we are so busy praying that we don't give God the opportunity to answer. Or perhaps we expect an answer that is huge and flashing across the heavens, when the actual answer is simply knowing that God listens and feels our pain, and struggles alongside us. Perhaps God is answering through another person. Perhaps the answer is simply God telling us to use the intellect we were given to work it out ourselves.

Young children learn best when they can work problems out themselves. If we hand them the answer for every problem, they don't grow in their ability to deal with the world. Even as adults, we learn from working out our own problems. That's when the real learning happens. That's when we really grow close to God, when we appreciate the gifts that God gave us to deal with our problems ourselves. That doesn't mean we are by ourselves in dealing with those problems, because God is forever with us. But it does mean that we sometimes must think for ourselves.

Reflect

~ When have you thought that God was not answering your prayers, and later realized that God was there with you all along?

~ When have you listened to another person and helped him or her simply let go and let God help with the problem?

~ What can you do to remind yourself to stop and listen to God?

Pray

Our God, I sometimes feel that you are far away and not answering my prayers. Help me recognize all the other people through our history who have felt this way. Give me the courage to continue praying, even when I fear that I am not being heard. Amen.

Lessons That Help Me Cry

Scripture: When Jesus saw that Mary and the people with her were crying, he was terribly upset and asked, "Where have you put his body?"
They replied, "Lord, come and you will see."

Jesus started crying, and the people said, "See how much he loved Lazarus."

—John 11:33-36

Grandchildren can sometimes be more observant of others' feelings than adults are. When we adults realize that someone is sad and on the verge of tears, we often ignore them, hoping that we'll not embarrass them. Or perhaps we're at a loss to help. We want to say something but are afraid we'll say the wrong thing.

At times I've been on the verge of tears for one reason or another, and invariably one of my grandchildren will climb up into my lap and help me cry. There is a real release when the tears can fall onto the head of a grandchild. They understand what tears are about. The younger ones certainly have no fear in showing their feelings.

Tears are natural products of feelings, and feelings are neither good nor bad. Feelings just simply *are*. Jesus affirmed our feelings when he cried over Lazarus with Mary. He knew that he would raise Lazarus from the dead, but rather than bolstering Mary up by telling her that everything was going to be all right, he simply wept with her. Jesus took the time to walk in her shoes and to feel her pain.

Recently, as my plane lifted off the runway and headed east out of Utah, I noticed that the young woman sitting beside me was on the verge of tears. I felt for her and wanted her to know that she need not be embarrassed. I found a packet of tissues in my bag and slid it across the lapboard to her. She mumbled a thank you, and we continued on our flight. A bit later she reached into her bag and handed me a paper. It was the program from the memorial service after her brother's death. She was returning from the funeral of this young man, whose life had been cut short by a motorcycle accident. We were able to talk together during the remainder of the flight, and she realized that a stranger could feel some of her grief. I silently thanked God that I had slipped the package of tissues into my bag that morning.

Sometimes helping someone feel the pain is the best thing that we can do in times of crisis. It makes a difference when we know that someone is there for us. I could cope better when my grandchild climbed into my lap and helped me cry.

Reflect
~ Who has helped you cry when you needed to?
~ When have you had the opportunity to help another person cry in a crisis?
~ When has a child shared a crisis with you?

Pray
Thank you, God, for those who care when we are in crisis. Help me be alert to those who need my listening ears and my accompanying tears. Amen.

Lessons of Generations

Scripture: A short time later Mary hurried to a town in the hill country of Judea. She went into Zechariah's home, where she greeted Elizabeth.

—Luke 1:39-40

It is exciting to observe the change in grandchildren as they approach their teen years. They often become much more interested in adult conversations. They pick up on what we are saying, even the subtle comments and our tone of voice. They are beginning to think for themselves and to separate their thoughts from those they have been handed in the past years.

Often children can turn to someone else more easily than to their parents when they have questions. They need someone who is a little removed from the situation. When Mary encountered the angel, she must have had some misgivings as to whether she could carry out this mission that God had entrusted her with. She needed to get away for a while to think things through. Elizabeth, a relative who was older and also expecting a child, was the perfect sounding board for Mary's thoughts.

There is a period in our developing faith when it is especially important to have clarifiers with whom we can talk. This usually happens during the mid- to late teens, and sometimes it doesn't begin until young adulthood. This is when we begin to take out the various beliefs that people have passed on to us, and we ask ourselves, "Is this what I truly believe, or is this only something that someone else has handed to me and I've accepted it without thinking deeply about it?"

We cannot truly mature in our faith and grow spiritually unless we are questioning our beliefs. Without questioning we are simply practicing a cookie-cutter faith. This is the time when we need clarifiers who say, "Some people believe in this manner, and others in that. What do you truly believe?" Then the clarifiers need to help the youth or young adult recognize that beliefs can change as we grow and mature in our faith.

Parents often find it hard to be those clarifiers because they are so close to the situation. That is when grandparents or another adult can be helpful. That is when we can be proud of our grandchildren's inquiring faith. We can know that without a clarifier to encourage the inquiring, the grandchild may turn away and give up on the church. They know that they need to think through these questions, but if the church tells them that such questioning is blasphemy, they may simply reject the church. Most often the inquiring leads right back to the training that they received as a child, but they must make it through the process for that belief to be firm. And if the belief changes, then we need to be right there to affirm their opportunity to inquire.

Reflect
~ What belief have you questioned in your life? Who helped you think through those beliefs?
~ How has questioning strengthened your own faith?
~ What grandchild or other youth or young adult can you develop a relationship with so that he or she feels comfortable to talk with you about faith matters?

Pray
Our God, I know that you are not disturbed with our questioning. Help me develop an open attitude that accepts the questioning of others, particularly those who are special to me. Amen.

Lessons of Encouragement

Scripture: You must encourage and help each other, just as you are already doing.

—1 Thessalonians 5:11

Whether the skill of encouragement is learned or is an instinct, I can't tell you. I'm no psychiatrist. I can tell you, however, that I've seen excitement in the eyes of children as they've applauded another child's actions.

With grandchildren of different ages, I've asked the older one to encourage the younger one in an accomplishment. However, when my twin grandchildren were learning to shoot baskets, I discovered one of them sitting beside me. She seemed to get as much joy from the act of clapping and encouraging the other one as she did when she took a turn at the basket. We had two balls, so they could shoot baskets at the same time. However, sitting beside me and clapping for achievement became as much a part of the game as shooting the basket. If the girl with the ball didn't make the basket, I'd hear the sister say, "Almost!" Then there would be a burst of applause. The girl at the basket would flash her sister a smile as she retrieved the ball and tried again. Once she made the basket, she'd turn to her sister and say, "Your turn." Then she'd take her sister's place beside me and become the encourager.

We forget that to be an encourager is a gift from God. Barnabas was considered an encourager. He encouraged Saul as Saul grew in the faith and became the missionary Paul.

When Paul became stable in his faith, Barnabas' mission seemed to turn to encouraging John Mark (see Acts 15).

As grandparents we can demonstrate the gift of encouragement. Children will recognize the way that we encourage them, and they will recognize the way that we encourage other adults. They will see that such actions are good and come about naturally.

I recall a time when a grandchild recognized a look of sadness in a parent's face and walked over to put an arm around the parent's shoulders. I recall the frequent words from the mouth of a young child, "What happened?" The tone of voice indicated more than curiosity. There was caring and concern. Things were not right, and the child seemed to long to do something about the problem. These acts are indications of the gift of encouragement, and we can nurture that. In our take-care-of-it attitude, we often forget to include the child. We see the child as an intrusion in our solution to the problem. We take on the attitude of, "I can do it myself!"; how much better to thank the child for the encouragement and concern. I think we all fail in this. I know I do.

Reflect
~ When have I seen a child encourage someone else?
~ When have I failed to nurture the gift of encouragement?
~ How can I demonstrate the gift of encouragement to children?

Pray
God, I often fail to recognize the gift of encouragement that you give us. Help me nurture that gift in myself as well as in others. Amen.

Lessons from Fear

Scripture: Don't be afraid. I am with you.
Don't tremble with fear. I am your God.
I will make you strong, as I protect you with my arm
and give you victories.

—Isaiah 41:10

It was a lovely day as we enjoyed the deck behind our house. My neighbor had stopped to visit for a few minutes. My two-year-old granddaughters were playing on the deck nearby when suddenly, for no apparent reason, one of them began to scream and rushed to me, climbing up my leg and into my lap. Of course this panicked the other granddaughter, and soon I had two screaming girls hanging around my neck and holding me as close as they possibly could.

My first concern was that she had been stung by a wasp, but there was no evidence of a welt. The only thing out of the ordinary that we could see was an innocent little lizard across the deck. Perhaps it had crawled across her leg and caused the panic.

As I reflected on the terror in my granddaughter's voice and eyes, I envisioned an image of God enfolding us in grandparent arms and soothing us during our panic attacks. What a privilege to stand in for our loving God and soothe the fears of two little girls.

My granddaughters rushed to me without hesitation. I wonder, however, if we will diligently train them to hide their fears as they become adults. Then they may bottle their fears inside, never expressing them to others and thereby never allowing others to minister to their needs. We stress the importance of standing alone to face our adversaries to such a degree that relying on others for support becomes a sign of weakness.

Our church has a program called Stephen Ministry, where persons are trained to support others in a crisis. The hardest part of that ministry is announcing it in such a manner that people feel comfortable asking for a Stephen Minister's help. We live in a world that affirms the statement, "I can do it myself!" We forget that Jesus gathered twelve disciples for support. Without the mutual support of that community, they never would have made it when Jesus left them.

I learned from my grandchildren that it's okay to turn for help to someone who cares. God put us in community, and in that community we support each other in our fears and traumas.

Reflect
~ What childhood experience can you recall that assured you of a parent's or grandparent's support in time of crisis?
~ What fear or crisis have you had recently where you've hesitated to ask for help?
~ What blocks you from seeking others who can help you in times of crisis and fear?

Pray
My God, I'm sometimes hesitant to ask for help. Remind me of the dependence of a child, and help me set free that childlike attitude of seeking help from others and from you. Amen.

Lessons of Forgiveness

Scripture: "I will go to my father and say to him, 'Father, I have sinned against God in heaven and against you.'"
—Luke 15:18 (from the story of "The Forgiving Father,"
Luke 15:11-32)

I'll never understand why some children quickly learn to say "I'm sorry," and others stubbornly keep their mouths closed. This seems to happen early on, and I'm not even sure they understand what the words mean. My grandchildren can be playing together, and one will accidentally bump the other and, as a matter of course, say, "I'm sorry." The other will say, "That's okay." But when the act was deliberate and it ends in tears, the child will stubbornly keep a closed mouth, even when urged to ask forgiveness.

Recognizing this helps me appreciate even more the story of the forgiving father, the parable that Jesus taught that is often called the parable of the prodigal son. It must have taken real courage for the young man to return to his father and ask for forgiveness. When we consider just how differently the young man and his older brother accepted responsibilities, we realize that it might have been easier for him to simply give up on life altogether than to lose face by returning home.

But perhaps he knew his father well enough to realize that he would be given a second chance, even if it was as a servant. This is why I like to name the story "The Forgiving Father." Such action of a Hebrew son, to ask for his inheritance early and then squander it, would have caused most fathers to disown the child. But instead, the father in Jesus' story was waiting for the son to return. The father must have been ridiculed by his neighbors as he paced up and down the road looking for his son's return. But he was Jesus' example of the father who forgave, even if it meant that he would lose face. This was an example of the true parenthood of God, the true meaning of grace—the loving and forgiving, no matter what.

And so my grandchildren help me understand this story better and help me appreciate the love and forgiveness that God offers us. No matter how far I stray from my responsibilities, and no matter how I must frustrate God with my actions, the love is still there for me.

Reflect

~ When have you admitted that it is okay to admit to being wrong?

~ When have you learned from your mistakes and asked for forgiveness?

~ When have you forgiven others, exhibiting the grace that is shown in this parable?

Pray

O forgiving Parent, I pray that I can learn from my mistakes—particularly that I can learn to ask for forgiveness. Help me show your love to others by offering forgiveness, even when it is not asked. Amen.

Lessons of Material Things

*Scripture: The rich may have to pay a ransom,
  but the poor don't have that problem.*

—Proverbs 13:8

Some people may feel that my grandchildren are deprived. They don't have the latest toys or fads. But their parents are caring enough not to give them everything that they want. When they were young, they didn't know of the things they did not have. An oatmeal box served as a drum, and a blanket on the stairs became a child-size sofa! They used markers (with the tops on) for flutes, a scarf became the train of a princess gown, and meals were served with imaginary food.

We have become so materialistic in our lives that we think we are not good parents or grandparents if we don't give our children the latest toy or the most recent technological invention. Television engrains these ideas with slick ads. Many parents work outside the home and see their children only for a short time at night and on weekends, and some grandparents live a distance away from their grandchildren. Consequently we try to make up for our absence by showering the children with gifts. If the child's friend has a special toy or game, then we think we must give our child something a little bigger and better.

In reality, the best gift we can give the children, besides our love, is an ability to use their imaginations, an ability to think for themselves. We can challenge them to create their own world of play and to see many different functions for one thing.

As I struggle to tame my desire to buy so many things for my grandchildren, I learn to pare down my own purchases and desires. I learn that I don't need the latest kitchen gadget when I have something else that can do the job with just a little more effort. I look around my house and realize that I have far too many collectibles to keep them dusted. I try to crowd another dress into my closet and realize that I have enough articles of clothing that I could go without washing for a month or more.

I begin to realize that more is not necessarily better. I begin to learn to live a stewardship lifestyle. I know that God has given me many gifts, and I have the responsibility to use those gifts wisely. There are others in the world who could use some of my gifts, and so I slowly learn to live simply so that others may simply live.

Reflect

~ What do you have in your house (besides seasonal items) that you have not used in the past six months? Can you get along without them?

~ How can you guard yourself against impulse buying?

~ With what item can you share ownership with a neighbor or friend so that you both don't need to purchase the same things?

Pray

I come to you, God, recognizing that the material world can easily get the best of me. I hear advertisements on television and see the lovely things my neighbors have, and I begin to feel deprived if I don't have these things myself. Help me learn to live a lifestyle of stewardship. Amen.

Lessons of Giving

Scripture: If we can encourage others, we should encourage them. If we can give, we should be generous. If we are leaders, we should do our best. If we are good to others, we should do it cheerfully.

—Romans 12:8

I think we are born as cheerful givers! It must be during our growing toward independence that we lose the cheerfulness in giving, and many people never get it back. When my grandchildren were young, I would give the child something, and he or she would examine it closely and then hand it back to me with a smile. I don't recall noticing this with my own children; however, I'm sure it happened. Maybe that's why God made the experience of grandparenting. At this age we are not as wrapped up in the rest of the world, and we can notice what's happening before our very eyes!

Recently I arrived home just in time for us to go to a restaurant to celebrate my upcoming birthday. I was behind schedule, and everyone was waiting for me. But the minute I came into the house, my twin granddaughters greeted me with excitement in their eyes and dancing in their toes. They pulled me around the corner to see the lovely planter that they had for my birthday. They wanted to see my reaction to their gift!

We often miss the opportunity to help children retain that cheerful attitude toward giving. One way to do this is to be deliberate in opening gifts and recognizing the giver with thanks. This is especially true at Christmas. We can help the child think ahead of time about how the gift recipient will react when he or she opens the gift, and then have everyone watch as the gift is being opened. Our response in receiving a gift also helps the child become a cheerful giver. When they see the joy in our faces, they recognize that they have done a good thing in giving the gift.

We find organizations asking us constantly to give, and their causes are usually worthwhile. But if we let our children see a negative attitude toward giving to these organizations, or a negative attitude toward being asked, they soon adopt that attitude themselves. We can make decisions ahead of time about the charities we will support and support them cheerfully. Then we can simply respond to other requests with a statement to that effect.

God has given us minds and bodies with which to carry out our jobs and earn money for our livelihood. In that manner, everything we own and all money we earn is really a gift from God. It is only right that we should give back some of what God has given us, and do it cheerfully. We should all become as little children in our joyful attitude of giving.

Reflect
~ How can you exhibit a cheerful attitude of giving?
~ What charities do you give to regularly? Have you investigated them and ensured that they are good choices?

~ How can you respond to a gift from a child in a manner that helps him or her attain a cheerful attitude of giving?

Pray

Giver of Gifts, help me be a cheerful giver and a cheerful receiver. Give me the wisdom to discern where my gifts should go and to keep this cheerful attitude before me. Amen.

Lessons of Mission

Scripture: Go to the people of all nations and make them my disciples.

—Matthew 28:19a

My mother was as dedicated a Christian as I've met. She saw her mission as following the challenge set forth by Jesus at the end of the Gospel of Matthew. In fact, when she was young, she was seriously concerned that all of the world would be converted to Christianity before she was able to go out as a missionary. O that everyone would follow Christ's example! What a difference it would make in this world.

I had no desire and felt no calling to go to far-off nations to spread the news of Christ, even though I did answer the call four times to go to other countries to train pastors and lay leaders in Christian education. I felt that my first calling was to raise children in the Christian way. In sharing that calling with other parents, I saw a need for books that would help parents. That began my writing career.

But it was not until my grandchildren came along that I really recognized what a mission we grandparents have right in our own backyards. We can influence those grandchildren in ways that even parents cannot. We have a completely different relationship with the children. We can stand back and see the whole picture. We are not as wrapped up in the stress of discipline and training.

But to accomplish this we must see our relationship with the children as a mission given to us by God. We must recognize just how privileged we are to have the opportunity to share God with them. That's what my grandchildren taught me— the importance of developing that relationship with them and then following God's leading.

For this mission there is no waiting to reap the rewards. Yes, we may have to wait years before we fully recognize the results of our relationship with our grandchildren, but the rewards come our way when a child flings himself or herself into our arms with squeals of joy! The reward comes when we burst with pride over an accomplishment or over the way that a child shares with another. The reward comes when older children draw pictures, placing you close to themselves in those pictures. The reward comes when we hear our grandchild negotiate with another child in a peaceful manner instead of flaring out in anger.

Christ may have sent his immediate disciples out into the world to spread his word, but Christ calls grandparents today, telling us that "all nations" includes the children who are our grandchildren.

Reflect

~ What challenge do you see as a grandparent sharing your faith?

~ When have you felt rewarded as a grandparent?

~ What opportunity can you use today to share God with a grandchild or another child?

Pray

Give me guidance, O God, as I share you and your word with children. Show me your ways of teaching, and guide me in your paths. Amen.

LESSONS OF THE UPS AND DOWNS OF LIFE

Lessons on Falling Down

Scripture: We gladly suffer, because we know that suffering helps us to endure. And endurance builds character, which gives us a hope that will never disappoint us.

—Romans 5:3b-5a

Oh, the lessons we can learn as we watch a grandchild learn to walk! The art of walking comes so naturally for adults that we forget what children must go through as they learn. I was told by my mother that she never let me crawl. The floors of our parsonage home were so rough that she feared I would have splinters in my knees. So I went from sitting to a walker, and from that to walking with a parent's hand, and then to walking alone. Recently I read that if we aren't allowed to fall during the process of learning to walk, we later have fears of falling. There is, undoubtedly, an art to falling down!

Most recently I watched my twin granddaughters learn to walk. It amazed me again just how many times they had to fall before they accomplished walking alone. Yet it never bothered them. They simply got up and tried again. Each fall taught them that a little more could be accomplished. Now they are into spinning until they become dizzy and fall on the floor laughing. They are teaching me that we can make brokenness into a journey of joy!

As adults we seem to be afraid to make a mistake. We think that life should be perfect. If we do make a mistake, we hide it or try to cover up. Then when we try again we often make the same mistake! We don't let the mistake become a lesson.

One of my mother's favorite sayings was the old proverb, "Don't cry over spilt milk." My grandchildren have taught me one better than that. They've not only taught me that crying over mistakes is useless, but they've taught me to go a step further and make that mistake into a stepping-stone to something better. We can learn from our mistakes and become better persons because of them.

In no way do I believe that God directs us into mistakes to teach us a lesson. God doesn't bring problems into our lives for a purpose. That is not the "will of God." *But*, God can use those mistakes and those problems for good if we allow it to happen. God can help us be much stronger persons with each mistake we make, with each fall we take in the process of learning to walk the path with God.

Perhaps the lesson that I've learned here should be titled "Falling Down Is a Way of Life." If we don't venture out and try, we will never learn to "walk" through life. We have a choice. We can either cry and try to cover up our mistakes, or we can use them as the steps in our new dance and dance our way into joy!

Reflect

~ What mistakes have you made that have helped you grow?

~ Where are you afraid to venture out for fear of making a

mistake? How can you overcome the fear of making mistakes?
~ What brokenness can you turn into a journey of joy?

Pray
*Help me, Lord, to look at the mistakes of life as stepping stones to a
more joyful life. Give me the wisdom to appreciate what you can do
with my life, even in its brokenness. Amen.*

Lessons on Decision Making

**Scripture: Don't be like the people of this world, but let God
change the way you think. Then you will know how to do
everything that is good and pleasing to him.**

—Romans 12:2

When our grandson was a preschooler we had a sort of game
that we would play when we visited together. He would say,
"What do you want to do, Grandma?" I would say, "I don't
know. What do *you* want to do?" Then he would say "I don't
know. What do *you* want to do?" And on it would go, until we
ended in giggles.

Sometimes decisions come easy, and sometimes they cause a lot
of stress. And sometimes the big decisions are easier to make than
the small ones. The type of decisions I sometimes have difficulty
making are decisions on my viewpoint about an issue. When
I'm confronted with such decision making, I may even lose
the ability to think clearly, or my decision may be simply an

emotional response. Emotions play a big role in issues. In fact, on occasion, emotions are the only criteria we use in such decisions.

Here are some helps that I've found useful in making decisions about issues.

1. Recognize that you do not need to hold an opinion on everything. If you are not well versed in the subject, wait until you are, or leave the decision making to others.

2. Look at both sides of the issue, and ask people *why* they hold specific positions.

3. Learn what is required in such a situation. Seek information from those not emotionally connected to this particular issue.

4. Recognize that you are entitled to your own decision, and make it according to your own findings and your own opinion on the issue.

5. Stand behind your decision all the way.

Make sure that you have followed a sound process in making your decisions on any issue and that you aren't taking someone else's word as your own.

For a Christian, prayer is important in any decision. Many of our church councils and committees have a prayer at the beginning and at the end of their sessions. I call these "book-end prayers." But there are times during a meeting when we should pray before a vote or before a decision is firmed. Don't be hesitant about asking that you take time during a meeting for prayer. The end results will be better for all involved if we bathe our decisions in prayer.

Reflect

~ What decisions are eminent in your life right now?

~ How have you applied the suggestions above to those decisions? How might you apply them?

~ What decision is before your church family now that needs to be bathed in prayer?

Pray

Our God, we can become so bound up in the stress of making decisions that we completely leave you out of the picture. Help us remember that your help should be at the center of any decisions we make. Amen.

Lessons on Whining

Scripture: When we were children,
  we thought and reasoned as children do.
But when we grew up, we quit our childish ways.
                                       —1 Corinthians 13:11

I recall a time when I took care of a couple of children for several days while their parents were elsewhere. The children were both of elementary age, and they whined most of the time when they asked for something or when something didn't go their way. I immediately told them that whining didn't work at our house. They had to speak in regular English if they wanted me to pay attention. This seemed to work (although I had to remind them periodically) until their parents returned. In a flash, the whining came back into their vocabulary.

As my grandchildren began to talk, I realized that whining was actually the pre-language of infants. Before they learned to form words, their vocalizing was very similar to the whines of preschoolers. These whines were actually their own language. Whining children seem to get what they want. But granting them their wishes doesn't stop the whining, because they learn that whining brings about their desires.

Perhaps we adults think that whining and constantly complaining will get us what we want too. The old adage of the squeaking wheel getting the grease holds true to some degree, but the person with the oilcan must hear the squeaking wheel. Often we do our whining and complaining to our friends and acquaintances who actually have no ability to make the changes. We complain about government; we complain about church; we complain about our jobs. But we don't complain to the right people. And we don't complain in the right manner. Our complaining sounds more like the whining of a child than the carefully formed statement of an adult. The whining is actually complaints, when it should be in the form of recommendations. These complaints usually have no positive suggestions. They just come across as whines.

Some years ago I heard a method for giving evaluations, which also makes sense for formal complaints. The suggestion used the image of a sandwich. By balancing our recommendations (formal complaints) with commendations, we make our evaluations more tasteful. The "sandwich" begins with bread (a commendation). Then we add cheese (concerns, not complaints). Now we are ready to add the meat (recommendation for change), and we also put on a bit of lettuce (let us rejoice!), and we top it off with another slice of bread (another commendation). By sandwiching the meat of the matter between two positive comments about the person or situation, it becomes more palatable. They know that we have thought through the situation and recognize the good as well as that which we believe should be changed.

Complaints, which are not placed in the right context and directed to the proper people, are simply whines that grate on the nerves. They even grate on the wrong people and set us up for a negative attitude about other things. If we are not going to step forward and do something positive about the problem, then we should just accept it the way it is without whining.

Reflect
~ What do you sometimes whine about on which you could take the initiative and do something?
~ What are some positive things about that situation that you could include in your suggestion for action?
~ How can you help others realize that whining without action is useless?

Pray
Dear God, we sometimes do need to come to you with our problems. Help us think them through and make steps where it is possible to do so. Amen.

Lessons on Frustrations

Scripture: Let the words of my mouth and the meditation of
my heart be acceptable to you,
O LORD, my rock and my redeemer.

—Psalm 19:14 (NRSV)

No matter how hard we try to keep our cool, there comes a time, while dealing with grandchildren, when we are on the verge of losing it! And sometimes, understandably, we do lose it. This most often happens when we are tired or when the children are tired. We can learn from those times, however.

It seems that I constantly say, "If only I could do it over." I regret what I said or did. Or perhaps it's what I *didn't* say or didn't do for my grandchildren. Anger continues to build in my heart, aimed at the grandchild and also at myself.

The prophet Nehemiah said that God is a forgiving God, gracious and compassionate, slow to anger and rich in love (see Nehemiah 9:17b). I am learning to apologize for my anger, even to apologize to my grandchildren. It seems strange that we, the "wise" grandparents, should apologize. But how else are the grandchildren to learn about the mistakes of anger? Not the mistake of being angry, but the mistake of the actions we take stemming from that anger. When we act in a not-so-wise manner, then we should become wise enough to learn from our mistakes and apologize. If we teach children that God is a forgiving God, then the anger and apology actually become a learning experience.

Usually the anger we have today will not make a bit of

difference five years from now, unless we act wrongly in the way we handle it. Anger is an emotion, neither good nor bad. Our problems come with the way we handle the anger.

According to the grandparent jokes, when we get angry or when the grandchildren are frustrated and angry we decide to give the children back to their parents. But that's not always possible. During these times of frustration I learn to depend on God to help me hold my tongue and use the situation as a learning experience.

Reflect

~ When have you been angry recently?

~ How can you see this situation as a learning experience?

~ What can you say or do that will trigger you to release that anger into God's care?

Pray

God, some days I want to rewind my actions and play them again, like the tape of a video movie. But I know that's not possible. I will move from this moment with your forgiving grace, and I know I will do better. Amen.

Lessons of Calm

*Scripture: **Losing your temper causes a lot of trouble, but staying calm settles arguments.***

—Proverbs 15:18

As the Nationwide commercials say, "Life comes at you fast!" At those times we become aggravated and ready to scream! It seems that everyone is pulling at us from all directions! We are in a whirlwind of emotions and on the verge of either melting into tears or exploding in anger. All too often we lose the battle and let our temper get the best of us.

I've seen this in a grandchild, and I have also seen it in myself when I've been dealing with grandchildren. (And at other times too!) With the grandchildren, such actions call for a "time-out." But with ourselves, we seldom take that "time-out" calming experience. We simply plow on through the day, becoming more and more angry with every little inconvenience.

God has given us the ability to stay calm and to temper our nerves. This is the part of ourselves that was created like God. This is the something deep down within us that can make a difference, not only in how we face the day but also in long-lasting relationships with others. But we must remain calm, or we must calm ourselves, in order to make use of it.

There are certain actions that I find helpful to use at such times. I'm sure you have developed some of your own.

Ron DelBene has shared the process of a breath prayer in several of his books. This is a prayer that can be said in one breath, breathing in and out. To create a breath prayer, DelBene suggests that you quiet yourself and imagine God calling you by name and asking you what you want. Then you answer God with one or two words, or a short phrase. Next, choose a favorite name for God. Combine your name for God with your answer to God's question, and this becomes your breath prayer. (*The Hunger of the Heart* [Upper Room Books: Nashville, 1992]). After you have done this on several occasions, you will have a breath prayer on the tip of your tongue to use when you become angry.

One common way people deal with anger is to slowly count to ten. When I get angry, I often ask myself, "Will this make a difference ten, twenty, fifty years from now? Is it that important?" The best action that I have found for dealing with anger, however, is to simply say to God, "All right, God, I need your help now, before I mess this up. I know that you can give me the calm I need." I will even admit to God that I simply can't go it alone. It's amazing how God comes through!

Anger itself is only an emotion, and having anger over something is natural. But how we react to the anger is a different thing. Actions out of anger never win the battle. They only set off a chain of events that escalates the anger and spreads it to those around us.

Reflect

~ In what ways do you deal with calming your anger?

~ Think of a time when you exploded in anger. How might you have handled it better?

~ How can you help children learn to deal with their anger?

Pray

Creator God, you know that anger can take over my actions at times. Help my control, and give me the calm that I need to deal with the aggravation of the moment. Amen.

Lessons on Troubles

Scripture: With all my heart I thank you.
  I praise you, LORD God.
Your love for me is so great
  that you protected me from death and the grave.

Proud and violent enemies, who don't care about you,
  have ganged up to attack and kill me.
But you, the Lord God, are kind and merciful.
You don't easily get angry,
  and your love can always be trusted.

—*Psalm 86:12-15*

My three granddaughters love to dance. They have swayed to music from the time they were able to pull themselves up to a table. When they are together, the oldest granddaughter finds dress-up clothing for the younger ones, and they are soon in their own world of dance. Even if they seem to be at odds with one another or with life in general, they can usually dance their troubles away.

I was well into my adulthood before I recognized how many of King David's psalms expressed his frustration with what was going on in his life and in the country. He was not hesitant to lash out at the Lord. David let God know just how he felt. But in each case, there followed a "but" or some other recognition of God's love and mercy.

Sometimes we fear telling God just how we feel about

situations. We hide our feelings as if they aren't worthy of presenting to God. We might even assume that they are sinful. Yet God made us with feelings. Those feelings are neither good nor bad. They are simply feelings. It is how we react to them that can be good or bad.

If we are to believe the Bible, we must recognize that it is legitimate to express our feelings to God. We can storm about, and rant and rave about all the negative happenings in our lives. The important thing is to follow David's example and also recognize that God is there for us, even when the bad things happen. In a way, that is like dancing our troubles away. We twirl like the whirlwind of our frustrations, and then we dance in joy over the fact that God continues to support us even in the midst of the bad. God loves with a happy heart and with a sad heart, but God continues to love.

God never promised that life would be easy. God only promised to be with us and to see us through.

Reflect
~ What negative things are happening in your life right now that you need to tell God about?
~ Where, in the midst of the darkness, do you see God's love shining through?
~ How can you express your love for God and your understanding that God is with you?

Pray
Dear God, sometimes I feel as though you have forsaken me. But then I realize that bad things come about because of circumstances,

not because you will them upon me. Give me the courage to express my feelings to you and the comfort of knowing that you care. Amen.

Lessons from Kite Flying

Scripture: I tell you for certain that before you can get into God's kingdom, you must be born not only by water, but by the Spirit. Humans give life to their children. Yet only God's Spirit can change you into a child of God. Don't be surprised when I say that you must be born from above. Only God's Spirit gives new life. The Spirit is like the wind that blows wherever it wants to. You can hear the wind, but you don't know where it comes from or where it is going.

—John 3:5-8

It was spring break. My daughter was free from her teaching obligations, so we gathered the twins and all the paraphernalia for two-year-olds and headed to the beach. The girls delighted in the sand and the ocean. At night they would look out the window and say, "Good night, Ocean. See you in the morning!"

Most of the days were very windy, but finally the day came that seemed perfect for kite flying. Now, I'm no expert on kite flying. In fact, when I was young, kite flying was a "boy thing," and we girls were allowed to hold the string only once the kite got up into the sky—if we were lucky, that is. I was never that lucky. Maybe I just didn't know the right boys, or maybe they thought my skinny body would not hold down the kite! But this day at the beach I watched the awe shining in two-year-old faces as the wind lifted the kite and sent it sailing across the blue sky and white clouds. What awe and mystery in God's world! So much to explore and learn about. And what a depth of religious symbolism is in store for these girls.

I understand that part of the art of kite flying is knowing just how much string to let out at the right time, and knowing when to pull it in and when to let it fly. It all depends on how you catch the wind. If you let out too much string too quickly, you cause a crash, but the kite dives if you hold on to the string too tightly when the strong winds burst out of nowhere. There's something about the distribution of weight, which I don't comprehend; but I understand that if it isn't right, it causes the kite to go in circles.

Once you get the kite up into the air, there are times when the string needs to be tightened if you want it to go really high. Then at the great heights, the kite can adjust to the conditions, as if it is one with the wind.

The Christian church has picked up on Jesus' reference to the wind as being like God's spirit. In the Book of Acts we read of the Holy Spirit coming to the disciples like a rush of wind (see Acts 2:2). The challenge of kite flying and the challenge of the Holy Spirit involves letting it take its own course, but sensing the movement that is happening and reacting to it appropriately. All of this is true, but what I learned most from my granddaughters on that windy day at the beach is to live in awe of the wind and its power over the kite. I must live in awe of God's power to lift me up and carry me above the strife of the world. Then I must respond to the Holy Spirit as it keeps me afloat.

Reflect

~ Where is the Holy Spirit tugging at your life?

~ Are you holding on to some things too tightly when the Holy Spirit could take you to greater heights?

~ How can you learn to be one with the wind and respond to the Holy Spirit with joy? Who can be your teacher in this kite-flying experience?

Pray

Help me, O God, recognize the awe of your presence. Lift me high and give me the burst of spiritual energy I need to go where you lead me. Let me see the potential of your power so that I allow it to move through me. Amen.

Lessons from Questions Asked

Scripture: One of the teachers of the Law of Moses came up while Jesus and the Sadducees were arguing. When he heard Jesus give a good answer, he asked him, "What is the most important commandment?"

Jesus answered, "The most important one says: 'People of Israel, you have only one Lord and God. You must love him with all your heart, soul, mind, and strength.' The second most important commandment says: 'Love others as much as you love yourself.' No other commandment is more important than these."

The man replied, "Teacher, you are certainly right to say there is only one God. It is also true that we must love God with all our heart, mind, and strength, and that we must love others as much as we love ourselves. These commandments are more important than all the sacrifices and offerings that we could possibly make."

When Jesus saw that the man had given a sensible answer, he told him, "You are not far from God's kingdom."

—Mark 12:28-34a

Who has not become bored with answering a child's questions? Children never seem to run out of questions. We tell ourselves, *"This is the way they learn,"* but the questioning can become old very quickly.

One thing I have learned, however, is that a child's questions mean that the child is thinking. Questioning children go beyond the edge of their knowledge. What they know no longer satisfies them. They search beyond the status quo. They want to continually push a little further. Their questions actually ask, What does that mean? How do you go on from there? What's the next possibility?

Perhaps we should follow the example of our children in our spiritual development. We begin our spiritual development with experience and affiliation with others. Each experience satisfies a bit of our need to know more about God. Each experience with God whets our appetite for the next. Each meaningful relationship with another Christian helps us see what God is like.

And then comes the time of inquiry. Others have shared their beliefs in God with us, and as we mature, we find a need to make those beliefs our own personal creed. We no longer feel that we can claim a belief just because someone else has told us, "It is so!" Now we must test it and make it our own. With this inquiring we become stronger spiritually; but if we hit an immovable wall where we are told that we cannot inquire into our faith, we often turn away and lose what ground we have already gained in our spiritual development.

We can grow when we ask questions. We stretch our hearts and our spirits. We are not content to simply accept the answers we had five years ago, or even a month ago. We need to forever look to new ideas and new understandings of God. These may just be a little different view or a deeper view of the image of God than we had before, or they may be drastically different. But if we allow it, the Holy Spirit will guide us through those questions, and we will find joy in the answers.

Just as a child can be happy with an inquiring mind, our souls can find happiness on the other side of our questions.

Reflect

~ What experiences of faith have you had in the past?

~ Who has influenced you in your understanding of God?

~ What questions do you now face when you think about your religious beliefs?

Pray

Dear God, there will be times when I have questions about my beliefs. I know that I must continue to look at the ways in which I understand you and ways in which you want me to live. I know that this must continue throughout my life if I am to continue to grow closer to you. Help me in my struggles. Amen.

Lessons of Learning

Scripture: "Moses and Joshua, I am going to give you the words to a new song."

—Deuteronomy 31:19a

Learning something new is commonplace for grandchildren, even when they are in their teens. During the child's first years the "new thing" is usually something that is very commonplace for grandparents. It may be learning how to hold one's head up, or it may be learning how to find one's thumb. Soon the learning includes sitting alone and walking and running.

As the grandchild gets older, the new things embrace learning how things work and discovering the awesomeness of God's world. Finally, our grandchildren learn what it's like to establish lasting friendships and to listen to God's direction for their lives.

As my grandchildren moved through each of these stages, I recalled again how important it is for me to embrace "new things." It is so easy to say, "That's the way it's always been, and if it was good enough for then, it's good enough for now!" It is hard to acknowledge that sometimes a new way is needed for a new time.

The people whom Moses led through the wilderness wished for the old country (Egypt) and the "old ways." They felt it was too hard to adapt to the new places, to the new relationships, to new songs, to the new understanding of God, even to their new freedom. When Moses went up into the mountain to encounter God, the people asked his brother, Aaron, for permission to build a golden calf-god like those they had seen in Egypt. The "new" idea of a God who was not visible was hard for them to embrace. Moses' displeasure in their actions was evident when he smashed the stone tablets with the laws God had given him.

The people of Isaiah's day were reluctant to see the new way. Yet God reminded them, through the prophet, that the best way might not always be the old "tried and true."

Jesus certainly encountered people who were not open to following the new way. He ran into conflict over the observation of the Sabbath, the understanding of forgiveness and love for one's enemies, the acceptance of children, the relationship with foreigners and people of different religions, even the commercial use of the courts of the Temple.

Jesus gave us a new way to look at revenge when he said, "When someone slaps your right cheek, turn and let that person slap your other cheek" (Matthew 5:39b). Just as Jesus taught us new ways to look at things, we need to learn that something tried in one situation (even if it seemed true then) may not be true in today's world. Each time, we must seek to find God's direction in the way we live our lives and the way we accept the past.

Reflect
~ What ideas of the past are you struggling with today?
~ Have you listened to what God has to say about new situations, or do you pray, simply pushing what you believe to be right?
~ To whom should you apologize because of your past stubbornness?

Pray
God of the past and God of the future, help me listen to your guidance in all things. Take away my stubbornness and give me a true understanding of your direction. Amen.

Lessons of Inner Peace

Scripture: Only God gives inward peace.

—Psalm 62:5a

Have you ever watched a baby with a full stomach sleep? I have had the privilege of watching four grandchildren sleep. There is nothing quite as peaceful-looking as a young child sleeping. There are no hard lines beside the eyes, no frown creases around the mouth. The only real concern that a baby has is that he or she be fed, and with that taken care of, the infant sleeps in peace. The body is completely relaxed. In fact, if you pick up a child who is in deep sleep, it can feel like you're holding a rag doll with no muscles at all. That must be the ultimate of inward peace.

How many times have I awakened in the night and not been able to go back to sleep? How many times in the morning have I felt my jaw muscles tense and tight? Why, I ask myself, can't I gain that inward peace that I see in the young child?

I recognize that God gives inward peace, but sometimes my actions (or lack of actions) block that peace. Sometimes I let my obligations slide and find myself pushing against a deadline, when originally I had plenty of time to complete the project. I've learned too well the art of procrastination! When that happens, God has difficulty pushing through and giving me the inner peace that I need.

Sometimes I've set goals (in time and in material goods) that are not realistic for me. At those times I spend restless nights and wrestle with tense muscles. I wake up tired and exhausted. I stay up late, exhausted but trying to finish the project. I seem to forget that God gave us the night to sleep. God could have made us so that we required no sleep. And so sleep is a gift from God, a way to gain inward peace.

It's easy for me, at a grandma age, to blame my sleeplessness and tiredness on age. In fact, that's often the answer that I hear from a doctor. But I know that the quietness of inward peace comes from God. I know that, even though I walk through the darkness of problems; even though I walk through the shadow of doubt; even though I walk through the obscurity of indecision; even though I walk through the gloom of failure—God is with me. I know, but so often I don't act on that knowledge.

Reflect

~ What can you do to ease the outward pressures that seem to block God's inward peace?

~ How can you change your routine at bedtime so that you are more relaxed, giving God the opportunity to soothe you through the night?

~ What problems do you have that can be released to God, giving you the inward peace that we see in a young child?

Pray

My God, it is with tense muscles and stressful thoughts that I come to you. I realize that your inward peace is available to me, and I know that I often block that peace. I now dedicate myself to making changes that will allow you to give me that gift. Amen.

LESSONS OF LOVE AND TRUST

Lessons on Trust

Scripture: But you, the Lord God, are kind and merciful.
You don't easily get angry,
   and your love can always be trusted.

—Psalm 86:15

How early do children learn trust? How do we build upon that trust? Why is it important to their spiritual lives that they trust?

These are some of the questions I ask myself as I consider the spiritual lives of my grandchildren. Then I recognize that we all trust in many ways. As I drive down the street, I trust that the driver approaching the intersection will stop at the red light. I walk into a hair salon and trust that my hair will be cut in the manner I request. I purchase meat at a supermarket or go to a restaurant and trust that proper health procedures are used. I leave my grandchild in an infant nursery and trust that the worker has been well screened and will care for the child.

Young children may not understand the concept of trust, but they begin early trusting in their caregiver for food and comfort. This early groundwork lays the foundation for a positive understanding of God. If children cannot trust those who care for them, whom they can see, then they have difficulty trusting God, whom they cannot see. And so I have learned that it is important for me to continually build trust with my grandchildren, no matter what their age.

I can do this by using the term *trust* and pointing out the situations where we trust other people and where we trust God. When the night comes, we trust that God will send the sun in the morning. When we place a seed in the ground, we trust that it will grow if we give it proper water and nourishment. When the fall wind blows and the trees begin to lose their leaves, I look for the buds that are on the limbs and trust that next spring those buds will burst forth into flowers or new leaves.

My grandchildren who are old enough to understand cause and effect can learn to trust in the laws of nature. If we let go of a helium balloon, it will float away from us. If we do not brush our teeth, we will have cavities. If we do not get our sleep, we will not function as well at school or at our jobs and are likely to get sick.

And if we pray, God will guide us to right choices. I don't want to instill an attitude of magic about prayer, but rather an understanding of prayer as a relationship with God.

My grandchildren are teaching me about trust, and I hope to be an instrument for God as they build on that trust.

Reflect

~ What were the opportunities for trust in your life today?

~ What situations of trust can you point out to your grandchild?

~ How do trust and prayer relate in your understanding of God?

Pray

Dear God, you are so much like a parent that I can trust. You will guide me, but yet you give me freedom to make my own choices. You seek opportunities to develop a deeper relationship with me. Thank you. Amen.

Lessons on Love

Scripture: I pray that [God] will help you live at peace with each other, as you follow Christ. Then all of you together will praise God, the Father of our Lord Jesus Christ.

Honor God by accepting each other, as Christ has accepted you.

—Romans 15:5b-7

Acceptance—how we seek it out. Children try to mimic adults in order to be accepted. Teens follow the current fad in search of acceptance. Adults worry about how they raise their children, eager to be accepted by other parents and also eager for the acceptance of their children. Sometimes these two rub against each other, causing sparks.

A favorite book of one of my granddaughters is *If Only I Had a Green Nose*, by Max Lucado and Sergio Martinez. I was familiar with their book *You Are Special*, so when I saw *If Only I Had a Green Nose* at my granddaughter's house, I had to read it. This series of books features the wooden people, the Wemmicks, and their relationship with their maker, Eli. This particular book tells about Punchinello's efforts to be accepted by painting his nose green. By the end of the book, Punchinello realizes that the color of his nose is not important. He can be himself, no matter what color everyone else paints their noses.

I know that my grandchildren will go through an age when they do some strange things in order to be accepted by their peers. In fact, it has already begun in some ways. As young as age two, the twins will mimic each other; and my older grandchildren have definite ideas about what they should wear to school. But I think they are learning to set limits on just how far to follow the crowd. By giving them choices within limits, and by giving them pride in their family principles, the parents of my grandchildren have helped them "save face" but still feel in control of their search for acceptance.

I don't know just what each grandchild will do in the future as he or she matures. I have no idea how they will act toward others, or what careers they will take, or whether they will excel in some particular area or be "generalists." I don't know whether they will marry and have a family or whether they will choose a single lifestyle. I only know that my love for them has become so strong that I will accept each one, no matter what she or he becomes. It may be that there are things that I don't condone, but I can still accept and love the grandchild.

And I know that God's love for them is even stronger than mine. God will love them unconditionally. God may love with a heavy heart sometimes, but God will continue to love. I've learned that this is the nature of God.

Reflect

~ What are some things that you may not like about a child's action but that you need to overlook?

~ What areas would you speak up about but still ensure the child of your love, even if you disapprove of the actions?

~ What can you do, apart from giving material gifts, to help that child recognize your love?

Pray

God, help me mimic the extreme love or grace that you give to each of us. Help me accept your grace for my life and pass it on to children as they mature. Amen.

Lessons on Communication

Scripture: Let my words and my thoughts
be pleasing to you, LORD,
  because you are my mighty rock and my protector.
                                                    —Psalm 19:14

I don't see my older grandchildren as often as I do my younger ones, and it always surprises me to discover how their communication skills have developed. I am particularly astonished when one of them sits down and carries on a conversation very much like an adult. It seems like only yesterday that they were babbling unknown sounds or asking the constant question, "What's that?"

It's interesting and sometimes frustrating to try to communicate with a newborn infant. Newborns don't even smile! Their only means of communicating is by crying. Of course, granted, they don't have much to communicate about. They usually cry when they are hungry or hurting in some way. Otherwise they mainly sleep.

Later, before learning words, the young child communicates with whines. Now, that's a communication that can really get on your nerves! Sometimes it's just a simple, "Ahhh, ahhh, ahhh!" But at other times it can become a high-pitched attempt at communication. It serves its purpose because it gets our attention, for sure!

As they reach the twos and threes, children learn to communicate with words, sometimes stumbling and sometimes repeating. Then the questions begin, and they continue throughout life.

As they grow older and their abstract thought progresses, children can express some of their innermost thoughts. Eventually, if allowed to question and ponder, they share deep discoveries with us.

Recognizing these stages has taught me something about prayer. Sometimes we can only cry out to God in our pain and in our need. In fact, that's usually the beginning form of prayer. We're often afraid to attempt a communication with the "powerful" God we've been taught about, and so it takes a real pain or need to force us to pray.

As we grow closer to God, however, we begin to stumble upon opportunities to express additional things to God. We also reach out to God with questions of why or when or how much. We begin to question just what God is like and how we can relate to this mystery around us.

It is only when we mature in our prayer life and recognize God as our close companion that we really open up and share our innermost feelings with God. Then we develop a one-on-one relationship with the powerful being that we call Creator, Protector, Rock, and Parent.

Reflect

~ How have you grown in your prayer life since childhood?
~ What sorts of things do you feel free to share with God in prayer?
~ What different images of God can help you express your innermost feelings to God?

Pray

I come to you in prayer, my God, but sometimes I feel I don't know how. I know that you want me to depend on you and to share my innermost feelings with you. Help me feel free to do just that. Amen.

Lessons of Our Heritage

Scripture: I also remember the genuine faith of your mother Eunice. Your grandmother Lois had the same sort of faith, and I am sure that you have it as well.

—2 Timothy 1:5

Our older grandchildren have learned the names of people from their past. Their parents display pictures of great-grandparents, aunts, uncles, and miscellaneous cousins. The children can name them and know something about the individuals. In fact, they even remember some of them. When I see the pictures or hear the children speak of them, I recognize what a blessed heritage they have! I also recognize what a responsibility I have to be a part of their faith heritage.

In his letter to Timothy, Paul wrote of the faith that Timothy inherited from his mother and his grandmother. Our faith heritage goes back not only through the family lineage but also into history through our faith lineage.

Abraham and Sarah stepped out in faith to follow God into a new land and establish a nation. Joseph's circumstances enabled him to save his family in the midst of famine, although he had to overcome any anger he had toward them for the way they had treated him in the past. The faith of Moses gave him the foundation for his remarkable role in rescuing the Hebrews from the Egyptians, even though he felt inadequate at first. In addition to building up the Hebrew nation, David wrote psalms that help us realize that it is okay to express our feelings to God. The prophets brought the people back to God with their words of warning. Jesus showed us what God is like and sealed our relationship, giving us assurance of eternal life. The apostles spread the word to those in other countries so that we all had opportunity to learn of the one true God. And there have been leaders and teachers since then, down through the centuries—leaders who taught us, and parents and grandparents who shared their faith.

Now we stand in that window of opportunity. Now each adult is a part of the timeline, or perhaps we should call it a storyline. We are primed to tell the story of our great faith heritage and thereby pass it on to the grandchildren. And it will then go on to their children and their children's children. And when all have heard, we will know that the Kingdom is surely complete!

Reflect
~ Who in your heritage has made a difference in your understanding of God?
~ What difference has that made in your life?
~ How can you make a difference in your grandchild's faith?

Pray
God of our parents, even if our parents did not accept you readily, we know that you were there, urging them and available for us. Give me the courage to step into the storyline of my faith heritage and take my place among those of the past. Show me how to share your story with children. Amen.

Lessons of Forgiveness

Scripture: Jesus called a child over and had the child stand near him. Then he said:
"I promise you this. If you don't change and become like a child, you will never get into the kingdom of heaven. But if

119

you are as humble as this child, you are the greatest in the kingdom of heaven."

—*Matthew 18:2-4*

Have you ever seen siblings who don't mildly disagree from time to time? Yes, sometimes the disagreement becomes more than mild. In fact, it can become quite angry. But I've seen two of my grandchildren disagree and then one of them turn to the other with a smile and a hug. When they were young, they couldn't label that hug as forgiveness, but that is exactly what happened.

Jesus must have known young children to have suggested that the attitude of a child is what we need in order to come into the Kingdom. As we get older, we tend to hold grudges longer. I'm not sure whether this is a learned trait, but adults hold those grudges much longer than children. Without God's love we let those grudges grind away at us, wearing us down until eventually we don't even remember what caused the rift between us.

Many of us who have worked or lived with children are familiar with the children's book *Love You Forever* (by Robert Munsch and Shelia McGraw [Firefly Books, 1986]). In this book the child's life is traced from birth to the end of his mother's life. The child's actions often seem to drive the mother crazy, but even when he pulls things off shelves and flushes his mother's watch down the toilet, she continues her same practice of love every night. When the mother is sure the child is asleep, she goes into his room, picks him up, and sings, "I'll love you forever, I'll like you for always; as long as I'm living my baby you'll be" (page 3). Perhaps this is why I like to think of God as a parent, a loving and forgiving parent.

God has given us the best model of forgiveness there is. God makes a covenant with the people, and continually the people break that covenant. They wander from God; they build golden calves; they plunder conquered countries when they are told not to; they give their gifts and sacrifices to the Temple without a true, repenting heart. Over and over again in the Old Testament the people went against God, yet each time God forgave them and found a way to come to the beloved children with a song of forgiveness. Sometimes that was through a prophet or a songwriter. Eventually God came to the people through a human experience, Christ.

God's forgiving love has been called *grace*. This is a word that I shied away from as a child. My encounter with the term was as a girl's name or in the hymn "Amazing Grace." It was my father's favorite song, but not mine. It was sung at too slow a pace! Now we have a more exciting version of the song, but I have also learned to appreciate the concept. I've learned that grace is a "love-you-anyway" type love. God loves with a happy heart and God loves with a sad heart, but God continues to love, no matter what.

Reflect

~ When have you seen the forgiving love of a child reflect God's love?

~ Whom do you hold a grudge against? How can you turn and become as a child in this situation?

~ Where do you need to forgive yourself? How do you repent or turn about and head in the right direction?

Pray

O Parent God, give me a forgiving heart. Give me a heart that forgives those who wrong against me, and also a heart that forgives myself. For I know that you love with a sad heart and with a happy heart, but you always love and will always love and forgive me. Amen.

Lessons of Peace

Scripture: It is truly wonderful
  when relatives live together in peace.

—Psalm 133:1

Sibling rivalry has been around for as long as we have had families, or perhaps we could say for as long as there have been people. The Old Testament verifies this. No matter how loving a family is, we still seem to experience times of disrupted peace within the family.

When our grandchildren fight with a sibling and then make up, I am reminded of Psalm 133:1. It *is* wonderful when relatives live together in peace. But how can we encourage that peace?

Of course with all children, *example* is one of the primary tools for teaching peace. If we cannot practice peacemaking as adults, we cannot expect our children to do so. Practicing conflict resolution can help bring about peace in the family. We can certainly do this when our grandchildren are with us. Here are some suggestions on how to practice conflict resolution:

- Set the stage in an affirmative way, choosing the right time and location for any discussion.
- In all discussions, use the terms "we" and "our."
- Agree to disagree on some things and still love each other.
- Clarify just where the disagreements are, who is involved, and just how important the disagreements are. Will this make a difference three years from now?
- In this conflict, what are the needs of each individual and of the family in general?
- Focus on togetherness instead of one person over another. Be positive.
- Learn from the past instead of punishing for the past. Look to the future in a positive manner.
- Look for common threads and goals, and creatively imagine options that will benefit all. Ignore preconceived answers.
- Set up steps of action that are "do-able" and can be agreed upon by all.
- Clarify responsibilities, and set about encouraging each other in action.

Just as children learn to walk and run by tripping and falling, we can learn peacemaking by learning from our mistakes.

Reflect
~ What peacemaking opportunities have you had lately? Did you take advantage of the opportunity or just let it slip by?

~ How can you use these suggestions for conflict resolution?
~ How did Jesus carry out peacemaking?

Pray
God of conflicts and peace, help me take advantage of every opportunity to model peace for those who look up to me. Amen.

Lessons of Family

Scripture: A body is made up of many parts, and each of them has its own use. That's how it is with us. There are many of us, but we each are part of the body of Christ, as well as part of one another.

—Romans 12:4-5

As my grandchildren came into my life, I learned to appreciate family in a greater sense. When our first grandchild was born, his parents diligently taught him the names of relatives, using pictures. The pictures were not in a photo album, but rather framed with importance and displayed on tables for the child to view. Our grandson later took pride in teaching his sister the names of the relatives.

Our daughter glued pictures on foam board and protected them with wide packing tape so that her young daughters can play with the pictures of relatives who are coming to visit, naming them as they play.

Watching our grandchildren view the pictures and hearing

them recite the names, I began to wonder just why we, in society, decided that independence in later life is so important. Did we have to create this myth to cope with our mobile lifestyle?

Sure, the Industrial Revolution caused young adults to move from the farm to the cities, but it was my generation that began the trend of seeing a move as a sign of adulthood. We eagerly cut the ties with family and prided ourselves on being independent. As we become senior adults now, we continue that trend. Although a few of us move in order to be close to our grandchildren, we often still cling together in "adult communities." Is this to prove our independence, or do we really want to be isolated from children?

As my grandchildren get older, I appreciate the importance of children having another adult, besides their parents, with whom they can talk and think through situations. Years ago the adult was the grandparent who lived down the block, or the aunt or uncle who lived nearby. Today these relatives may live too far away for quick conversations. E-mails and phone conversations can be used instead, but unless a relationship has been established ahead of time, the e-mails and phone conversations remain artificial. Our family just experienced several days of a combination fiftieth anniversary and family reunion. Cousins renewed friendships and realized that the years between their ages shrank as they became adults.

When renewals and new family relationships come about, memories are shared and relationships deepened. As my grandchildren have taught me, I seek to deepen these relationships that are so important.

Reflect

~ How well do you know the members of your extended family?

~ How do you maintain ties with your extended family? What difference will it make for them and for you?

~ What children do you know who could use another adult to talk to? How can you become better acquainted with those children?

Pray

Dear God, give me the opportunities to act as a caring adult for my grandchildren and other children in my life. Bring those children close, and give me wisdom to know ways to build the bridges for communication. Amen.

Lessons on Help Requests

Scripture: Show me your paths and teach me to follow;
*   guide me by your truth and instruct me.*
You keep me safe, and I always trust you.

—Psalm 25:4-5

Everyone expects babies to cry for help. Their helpless bodies bring out our concern. Their loud cries demand our attention. And they're so cute we can't resist helping them anyway!

Even older children need help from time to time. It pleases us grandparents to be able to help them with homework. This is especially so when the subject is one that we remember! At other times we are somewhat lost and realize that the young kids know more than we do!

But what about when grandchildren become young adults and "should know about that"? How do we feel about their cries for help then?

God has worked with people for many years, giving us help and instruction. But sometimes we just don't seem to get it! We flounder, or we just plunge into it, never trying to discover and follow God's direction. The human element of God must get exasperated! Yet God continues to pick us up as a people and dust us off, and send us out again.

As I answer my grandchildren's pleas for help, I can remember that God also answers *my* requests for help. God may not make things happen just the way I would like for them to happen. But God is always there to help us in the bad situations as well as in those that are good.

Many of the grandchildren's cries for help are simply requests to help them make decisions. Perhaps these questions will help as you and your grandchildren listen to God in your choices:

- Does this choice help me grow in my partnership with God?
- Does this choice turn me away from God?
- Am I claiming this choice as God's will simply to justify what I want to do or what someone else wants me to do?
- Are my actions truly prompted by God, or by what others will say or think about me? (from Delia Halverson, *Living Simply, Simply Living* [Nashville: Abingdon Press, 1996], page 20)

Reflect

~ Whom do you know who needs your help but seems hesitant to ask? How can you ease the bridge between this person and you so that your help is accepted?

~ When have you last turned to God for help? When have you ignored God when you really needed the help?

~ What help do you need from God right now?

Pray

Dear God, you instructed the psalmist in his paths long ago. I know that you continue to offer help to each of us. I now open myself to that help. Amen.

Lessons in Adoption

Scripture: You have received a spirit of adoption. When we cry, "Abba! Father!" it is that very Spirit bearing witness with our spirit that we are children of God.
—Romans 8:15b-16 (NRSV)

Before our daughter began the process, I knew very little about adoption. I knew that it was all done through the courts, but I had no idea that there was so much paperwork and so many requirements. As she worked through the procedure, I began to reflect on the statement that Paul wrote in his letter to the Romans.

First I realized just how much our daughter wanted a little

girl, which ended up being two (twins)! She felt that this was a part of God's calling, for her to raise a child. It reminded me that we are desperately wanted to be involved as children in God's family.

Then our daughter had to make the selection of an adoption agency. I realized that God didn't need to choose, because God has the capability of loving each and every one of us. God's love is beyond our human limitations of financially caring for a certain number of children. God already has provided everything we need in this world, although we often thwart God's plans and don't share God's gifts evenly among ourselves.

After the initial paperwork, our daughter had to have a number of visits by a certified social worker to determine that the home situation was suitable for the child, and then she had to have a criminal background check. Now, that's one area we don't have to worry about in our adoption by God. We know that God is the best possible parent there is. We have the Bible as a character reference for God, as well as a record of all of those people in the past who have been adopted into the family of God.

Then we went to pick up the tiny girls, and it was love at first sight. Our daughter knew that these precious children were hers, even though we had only met them that evening. God, however, has known each of us from the time we were conceived in the womb. God has adopted us, and we are forever in the family of God.

Some time later the final adoption papers were signed. Then the girls' birth certificates were changed to reflect our daughter's name, and the girls were granted all of the privileges of a natural child, including inheritance rights. We, as adopted children of God, receive the inheritance of eternal life through Jesus' death and resurrection. God has provided, and we are God's, forever and ever.

Reflect

~ How do you feel about being adopted into the family of God?

~ What responsibility to other children of God does such a relationship mean to you? How equal do you feel with other siblings in God's family? What sort of action is called for if we are truly equal siblings?

~ How should you act toward God when you recognize that you are a true child of God?

Pray

O Parent-God, I marvel that you want me in your family and that you loved me even before I was born. Help me act as a true member of your great family. Amen.

Lessons on Sleep Patterns

Scripture: I can lie down and sleep soundly because you, LORD, will keep me safe.

—Psalm 4:8

As I looked in on my two older grandchildren, I appreciated the peacefulness of sleep. It had been a busy day. They were visiting with us, and the day had been filled with swimming and playing with their cousins. Oh, there had been arguments, as there always are, but all in all it had been a successful day. Now they lay sleeping, and there was nothing but peace on their faces.

I was reminded of the words of the psalmist. Just as my grandchildren knew that they were safe in Grandma's house, we know that we are safe in God's care.

I cannot guarantee unconditionally that no harm will come to them in my house. I will do everything I can to keep them safe, but some freak accident could happen. A tree could fall through the roof of their room, or lightning could strike the house.

In the same manner, when we speak of being safe in God's care, we realize that it doesn't mean that we will never have problems. It doesn't mean that God will physically protect us from adverse weather. And it doesn't mean that God will divert a drunk driver so that our car is not hit. But it means that God will be with us no matter what the circumstances.

I've also learned from the peaceful sleep of my grandchildren that God uses sleep patterns to renew our bodies. As the grandchildren grew older, their sleep patterns changed. When they were very young they slept more than they were awake. Then they settled into two nice naps a day. At one point it was a struggle for them to adjust from two naps to one longer one. When their bodies had growth spurts, they slept more.

Now at the grandma age, I find myself awake in the middle of the night. After I toss and turn for a while, I remember that I can trust God for sleep. God uses sleep to renew us, and when I release my thoughts and relax my body, I succumb to a peaceful sleep too.

Reflect

~ When are you most likely to feel stressed and unable to sleep?

~ What eases the tension in your body?

~ How can you recognize that God gives you a peaceful sleep?

Pray

Dear God, my life becomes hectic, and too often I take that stress to bed with me. Help me relax and recognize that you give me the gift of sleep. Amen.